UNSUNG PILLARS OF THE UNIVERSITY OF SCRANTON

D1523035

UNSUNG PILLARS OF THE UNIVERSITY OF SCRANTON

Rodney L. Kelley

Unsung Pillars of the University of Scranton

Copyright © 2023 Rodney L. Kelley

All rights reserved. No part of this publication may be reproduced, distributed or transmitted in any form or by any means, including photocopying, recording, or other electronic or mechanical methods, without the prior written permission of the publisher, except in the case of brief quotations embodied in critical reviews and certain other non-commercial uses permitted by copyright law.

Unsung Pillars of The University of Scranton / Rodney L. Kelley
ISBN: 9798864561096

DEDICATION

This book is warmly dedicated to Robert J. Burke, a beacon of dedication whose hands, heart, and discerning eye shaped the spirit of the University of Scranton for 35 years. In the following pages, the biographical tapestry of those who serve beyond the spotlight owes its richness to his legacy. Each vignette is a life he touched; every narrative is a testament to his unwavering commitment to the ethos of this institution.

An alumnus, a veteran, and a recipient of the Pro Deo Et Universitate award, Robert's story is interwoven with that of the University itself. His devotion extended beyond the campus to a life rich in love, a marriage partnership that stood the test of time, and now rests in the hallowed ground of Mount Carmel cemetery in Dunmore, Pennsylvania.

Unsung Pillars of the University of Scranton

To the man who, behind the scenes, saw the promise in each individual, this book is a tribute to the indelible mark he left on the University of Scranton and its people. We stand as stewards of his vision, a community forever grateful.

TABLE OF CONTENTS

Chapter One

The Heart of the University of Scranton:
Tales from a Summer Spent Amongst its Pillars

Unsung Pillars of the University of Scranton

In the mid-1960s, a time of cultural and social transformation, the bulletin board in the student center at the University of Scranton in Pennsylvania was a collage of collegiate life, brimming with notices. A young man's eyes were drawn to a unique summer job posting among them. It was an era when the winds of change were blowing, and students yearned for experiences that offered more than just a paycheck—they sought roles that could add meaning to their lives. This job promised precisely that.

Student Center

The role was atypical; it required a student to be a jack-of-all-trades, stepping into various administrative and staff positions as employees went on vacation. For the student, it was an intriguing proposition. It meant a summer of walking in different shoes, gaining a kaleidoscope of experiences across the university's operational spectrum.

This opportunity was more than just work; it was a ticket to the behind-the-scenes world of the university—a place where the gears of daily operations were turned by those who often worked in the shadows. The young man saw this as a chance to dive into

Unsung Pillars of the University of Scranton

the heart of the university's ecosystem and emerge with a richer understanding of the community he was part of.

The University of Scranton, with its Catholic heritage and regional influence, was more than its stately architecture and manicured lawns. It was a community sustained by the dedication of its support staff: janitors, secretaries, kitchen workers, and maintenance crews. These individuals were the unsung pillars of the university's life, performing essential tasks that, while critical, seldom garnered public recognition.

As the summer unfolded, the student began his journey through the university's various departments, discovering the silent yet vital contributions of the support staff. The janitors, who ensured every corner of the campus, gleamed. The secretaries, whose organizational skills kept the administrative wheels turning smoothly, and the kitchen staff, whose culinary efforts nourished the body and soul of the campus community, even when most students and faculty were away.

Each new role brought the student face-to-face with the realities of these workers' lives—their challenges, joys, and pride in their work. He learned about the quiet satisfaction they felt when a task was well done and the sense of purpose, they drew from being part of the university's mission. He also saw the personal sacrifices they made, often unnoticed, to keep the university a place of learning and growth.

This immersive experience revealed the interconnectedness of all roles within the university. It showcased the harmony required between every institution member to maintain the standard of excellence Scranton was known for. The student realized that the university's heartbeat was steady because of the people who cared enough to ensure its rhythm never faltered.

Unsung Pillars of the University of Scranton

By the time the leaves began to turn and the academic year beckoned, the student had been profoundly affected by the summer's lessons. He had learned that acknowledgment and appreciation of everyone's work, regardless of the role, were vital to the health of any community.

This narrative of a young man's summer job reflects the spirit of the 1960s—a time when seeking purpose and making a difference were at the forefront of the younger generation's minds. His experiences at the University of Scranton were a microcosm of this broader societal shift, encapsulating the desire to connect with and contribute to the community meaningfully.

Historians often say that history is the story of people, and the true essence of the University of Scranton lies not just in its physical structures or academic achievements but in its people— all of its people. This includes the support staff; whose commitment and quiet perseverance became integral to the university's narrative. Their stories, while perhaps lesser known, are no less a testament to the character and spirit of the institution.

In the years that followed, the student, now a graduate, carried the lessons of that summer with him. The work ethic, resilience, and integrity of the staff he worked alongside became benchmarks for his life. He saw the value in every role and the importance of every contribution, no matter how seemingly small. The summer job had been a revelation, teaching him that the grand narrative of history is composed of countless smaller stories, each significant in its own right.

The legacy of the University of Scranton, therefore, is not merely an academic one. It is a legacy of people: from the faculty who teach to the staff who support, from the students who learn to the alums who lead. Each person contributes a verse to the ongoing poem, the university's history.

Campus Entrance

As the former student looked back on his days at Scranton, he appreciated that his education had come from textbooks and lectures and from the stories and lives of those who kept the university functioning. The summer of 1967 was more than a season; it was a chapter of growth, a passage of learning beyond the classroom, where the silent dedication of many painted a vivid picture of what truly makes an institution great.

This reflection on a summer job is more than nostalgia; it is a recognition of the collective effort that forges the identity of an institution. It is a celebration of every person who contributes uniquely to the tapestry of life at a university. For the student, it was a foundational experience that would inform his understanding of the world and his place within it for years.

Unsung Pillars of the University of Scranton

Chapter Two

The Quiet Force of Faith

Unsung Pillars of the University of Scranton

2.1 America's Catholic Colleges in the Mid-20th Century

In the sprawling tapestry of America's educational landscape, the mid-20th century held a unique place for institutions forged in pursuit of academic excellence and the crucible of faith. These were the Catholic colleges and universities, steadfast beacons of higher learning, where the flame of knowledge was kindled within the walls of tradition and spiritual guidance.

Over two hundred such institutions dotted the vast expanse of the United States, each one a testament to the enduring legacy of Catholic education. They stood as fortresses of learning, where thousands of young minds embarked on their intellectual journeys, nourished by rigorous academia and deep-rooted spiritual values.

Among these, a distinct group emerged, carrying a legacy that traced to the tumultuous days of 16th-century Europe: the Jesuit colleges and universities. Founded by the Society of Jesus, an order established by the visionary St. Ignatius of Loyola, these 28 institutions were the torchbearers of an educational philosophy transcending mere bookish knowledge. The "Ratio Studiorum," as it was known, was not just a curriculum but a way of life. It championed the holistic development of students, ensuring they emerged not just as scholars but as conscientious citizens, deeply aware of their roles in a world much more significant than themselves.

The corridors of Jesuit institutions echoed spirited debates on literature, philosophy, and the sciences, underpinned by a commitment to social justice and service. These colleges, from the bustling streets of the East Coast to the sun-drenched expanses of the West, gained a reputation not just for their academic prowess but also for molding "men and women for others."

Yet, every institution, no matter how hallowed, has its challenges. The public's perception of these Catholic and Jesuit institutions was a mosaic of admiration, skepticism, and sometimes misunderstanding. Controversies arose, shaped by the tides of time, societal changes, and the ever-evolving relationship between Church doctrine and modern thought. But through it all, these institutions remained undeterred, their foundations firm in the belief of greater purpose.

As one delves into the story of America's Catholic colleges in the mid-20th century, they were not just centers of education. They were crucibles where the nation's future was shaped, young minds were nurtured, and the quiet force of faith left an indelible mark on the annals of American history.

Unsung Pillars of the University of Scranton

2.2 The University of Scranton: A Testament to Tradition and Tenacity

In the heart of Scranton, Pennsylvania, stood a beacon of Catholic education–the University of Scranton. Amidst the myriad of over two hundred Catholic colleges and universities that marked the mid-20th century American landscape, Scranton held its own with pride and purpose.

During these formative years, the University had an intimate composition that starkly contrasted with some larger Catholic institutions. The faculty, a dedicated assembly of a educators, were not mere instructors but mentors who guided their students through academic endeavors and life's many challenges. Their commitment was evident in the tight-knit community they fostered, where each student was more than just a roll number; he was an individual with dreams, aspirations, and potential.

The student body thrived in the low thousands in this environment. Here, in the corridors of Scranton, they weren't lost in a crowd but stood out, each carving his niche. This cohort brought together young minds from various walks of life, united under the banner of Jesuit education. Rigorous academic pursuits shaped their days, underpinned by the principles of the "Ratio Studiorum," as well as lively extracurricular activities, which solidified bonds of brotherhood.

Set against the backdrop of Scranton, a town pulsating with dynamic energy, the University reflected a synergy of tradition and progress. While the town's ethos of hard work and perseverance seeped into the University's culture, the institution contributed immensely to Scranton's intellectual and cultural vibrancy.

Unsung Pillars of the University of Scranton

In this setting, the students and faculty of the University of Scranton navigated the challenges and triumphs of the mid-20th century. Together, they crafted a legacy that was not just about academic excellence but also about shaping men of character, men "for others."

In the grand narrative of Catholic higher education in America during this era, the University of Scranton carved a special place with its modest size yet immense spirit. It stood as a testament to what a community bound by faith, tradition, and commitment to excellence could achieve.

Unsung Pillars of the University of Scranton

2.3 An Ode to the Academic Community of Mid-Sized Catholic Institutions

In the heart of America's vast educational expanse, the mid-20th century painted a vivid tapestry of academic institutions, each with its unique ethos and character. The mid-sized Catholic colleges and universities held a special place for their scale and the intricate dance of roles and responsibilities that made them tick.

At first glance, one might be drawn to the towering figures of academia–the erudite professors with their profound knowledge and passion for shaping young minds. Their classrooms echoed with spirited debates lectures that inspired and the persistent quest for truth. Alongside them, the diligent students, hungry for knowledge, charted their paths, their futures intertwined with the institution's fabric.

Yet, in the shadows, ensuring the seamless flow of this academic dance, were the unsung heroes–the support staff. Theirs was a role often overlooked, but without which, the essence of the academic community would crumble.

The librarians, custodians of knowledge, ensured generations of students had access to the vast repositories of wisdom. They were more than just keepers of books; they were guides, helping many navigate the labyrinth of literature and information.

Administrative staff, often the first point of contact for many students, ensured every process was smooth, from admissions to graduations. They were the bridge between students and faculty, handling logistics with a finesse that often went unnoticed.

Unsung Pillars of the University of Scranton

Maintenance and janitorial teams worked tirelessly, often after hours, to ensure that the sanctity of the academic environment was preserved. Their dedication ensured that lecture halls were pristine, laboratories were in order, and the campus echoed the dignity of its purpose.

The kitchen staff provided nourishment and a sense of home in the dining halls. Their meals, often cooked with love and care, comforted many who were far from their families.

In the intricate ballet of academia, while faculty and students were the visible performers, the support staff was the stage, the backdrop, the lighting, and the music. Their roles, though diverse, converged towards a singular purpose - ensuring that pursuing knowledge went on unhindered.

In the grand narrative of mid-sized Catholic colleges of the mid-20th century, each community member played their part to perfection. While accolades often went to the luminaries of academia, the true strength of these institutions lies in the collective spirit of everyone involved, especially the unsung pillars who supported them.

Unsung Pillars of the University of Scranton

2.4 Scranton's Work Ethic and Its Echoes in University Halls

The mid-20th century bore witness to a town that pulsed with an energy both indefatigable and distinct: Scranton, Pennsylvania. Known as the "Electric City," Scranton's heartbeat was its dynamic spirit, an ethos forged in its coal mines' furnaces and reverberated in its railroads' rhythms. This was not merely a town but a testament to the American dream, where grit, determination, and commitment to honest labor were the cornerstones of existence.

Every alley, storefront, and home in Scranton echoed stories of hard work and families who believed in the dignity of labor and the promise of a better tomorrow. This work ethic was not just about economic survival; it was a badge of honor, a legacy passed down generations, shaping the character of every Scrantonian.

Nestled within this dynamic landscape stood the University of Scranton, an institution that was a microcosm of the town itself. Just as Scranton was more than its mines and railroads, the University was more than its lecture halls and libraries. And integral to its spirit and function were the support staff, the unsung heroes who ensured the academic machinery ran smoothly.

Much like the broader Scranton community, the support staff of the University of Scranton imbibed and exemplified a work culture rooted in diligence, pride, and a deep sense of responsibility. They were not mere employees but custodians of an institution representing hope, knowledge, and progress.

Unsung Pillars of the University of Scranton

The janitors, administrative clerks, librarians, and kitchen staff approached their roles not just as jobs but as a vocation. Their commitment mirrored the miners' dedication to extracting coal, the precision of the railroad worker in laying tracks, and the attention to detail of the factory worker. Every polished floor, every well-maintained bookshelf efficiently handled the administrative task, and every warm meal served was a testament to their dedication.

In the university corridors, stories were often shared about how a janitor would work late into the night to ensure classrooms were spotless or how an administrative staff member went above and beyond to assist a student in distress. These tales were not mere anecdotes but emblematic of a culture where work was both duty and devotion.

The work ethic of Scranton, forged in the fires of industry, found its reflection in the hallways of the University of Scranton. With their unwavering commitment, the support staff stood as pillars, echoing the town's values and ensuring that the University, much like Scranton itself, remained a beacon of hope, perseverance, and relentless pursuit of excellence.

Unsung Pillars of the University of Scranton

2.5 Of Service and Sacrifice

The sprawling mosaic of figures who have built and nurtured its legacy is rich in the University's panorama of Scranton's storied past. To the casual observer, the prestigious faculty dominate the foreground with their doctorates and robes. Yet, those with a discerning eye will notice the figures who operated quietly in the shadows, those uncelebrated individuals who were integral to the narrative but were seldom acknowledged. At the heart of Scranton in the 1970s, there was such a group: the staff and administrators. Their story is quiet dedication, service beyond the call of duty, and a commitment anchored not in financial reward but in a calling of higher purpose.

To truly understand the University, one must discern the distinction between faculty and staff/administrators. The faculty, ever in the limelight, bore the responsibility of imparting knowledge, molding young minds, and contributing scholarly research to the academic community. Their positions were often tenured, providing them with security and benefits. Their expertise and dedication, rightfully so, brought acclaim to the University and established its reputation as an esteemed seat of learning.

Yet, just a few steps behind these learned individuals were the staff and administrators, the institution's backbone. Their duties, though less publicized, were no less significant. They ensured that the University's operations ran seamlessly, from managing the enrollment of students and maintaining the campus's lush green landscapes to guaranteeing that each facility was equipped and ready for the faculty and students. The silent gears, seldom recognized, kept the University machinery running smoothly.

Unsung Pillars of the University of Scranton

The stark difference lay in recognition. While the faculty were celebrated in terms of prestige and compensation, the staff and administrators often remained in the shadows. Their modest remunerations, however, did not reflect the countless hours they poured into their work. Yet, it wasn't the allure of financial rewards that kept them devoted. The University of Scranton, steeped in its Catholic roots, instilled in them a sense of purpose, a vocation, a calling. Their work wasn't merely a job; it was a mission.

For many of these unsung heroes, the University became a lifelong commitment. They spent decades in service with little public acclaim or fanfare. But, true to their character, they sought neither. Their rewards were more intangible: the satisfaction of a job well done, the knowledge that they played a crucial role in the educational journey of countless students, and the silent prayers whispered in the campus chapel, hoping for the University's continued success.

In the following pages, we will profile each of those dedicated staff and administrators listed in the 1972 edition of the University of Scranton Windhover yearbook. While others deserve this recognition, a comprehensive listing is unfortunately not available. These individuals represent all who gave their careers, passion, and commitment to serving the university community.

To honor the faculty is just, but to overlook the staff and administrators is an oversight we must rectify. In the early 1970s, as the University of Scranton grew and evolved, these individuals gave of themselves wholeheartedly, often expecting little in return. It is time they take their rightful place in the annals of the

Unsung Pillars of the University of Scranton

University's history, for without them, the story remains incomplete.

History reminds us that the vast dark matter holds the universe together while the stars shine brightly. The staff and administrators of the University of Scranton are that essential dark matter - unseen, uncelebrated, but undeniably indispensable. Their legacy is a testament to service, sacrifice, and an unwavering commitment to an institution they held dear. For their contributions, they deserve our deepest gratitude and respect.

PERSONNEL
OF
THE COMMUNITY

Windhover Yearbook
University of Scranton
1972

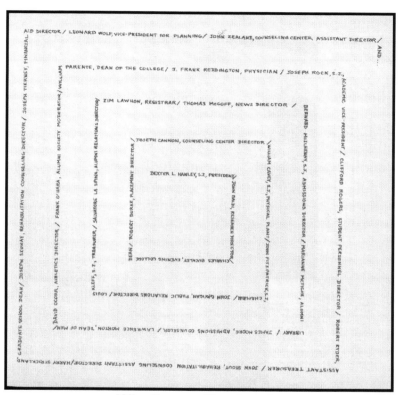

Windhover Yearbook
University of Scranton
1972

Unsung Pillars of the University of Scranton

Halls / MARY GALLAGHER, Admissions Office / LOUIS GALLO, Long Center / ROSE MARIE GRAMBRONE, Estate / VIRGINIA GILROY, Book Sellers / GENE LOMBARDO, Residence Halls / STANLEY GARSKI, Loyola Hall / MADELYN GORSLINE, Residence Halls / ROBERT GIRAMBO, Student Center / ROYCE GRECO, Athletics Office / RAY GREGOS, Cafeteria / ETHEL GRIMES, Cafeteria / EDWARD HAWLEY, Carpenter / JOSEPH HROBAN, Library / HAROLD HOMER, Long Center / ANN HOPKINS, Residence Halls / ANN HOSKINS, Public Relations

and Development / GEORGE HODUK, Long Center / MARY HYLAND, Graduate School Office / THERESA JASHENSKY, Residence Halls / JOHN JOYCE, St. Thomas Hall / ROSALIND JOYCE, Registrar's Office / FRANK KANE, Residence Halls / PETER KAPP, Long Center / JOSEPH KAVBLNES, Cafeteria / CATHERINE KELLY, Residence Halls / DOROTHY KENNEDY, Registrar's Office / MARTIN KLEPADLO, St. Thomas Hall / WILLIAM KNELLER, Long Center / STEPHANIE KOWALSKI, Residence Halls / MARIE KOZIK, Rehabilitation Office / LEO KUPLINSKI, Student Center /

ABBEY ABBOTT, Library / GARY ACKERMAN, Treasurer's Office / GERALD ALLEN, Student Center / PATSY AMORE, Estate / MICHAEL BALENDY, Residence Halls / KATHLEEN BARRETT, Computer Center / MARGARET BASS, Residence Halls / LLOYD BEAM, Long Center / RITA BELLAS, Cafeteria / JUDITH BLACK, Financial Aid / FRANK BLOOM, Cafeteria / GEORGE BODMAR, Mail Room / JEANNE BRACK, Print Shop / JAMES BROWN, Bookstore / EDWARD BUCHALSKI, Residence Halls / JAMES BURNS, Cafeteria / ROSEMARY BUTLER, Evening College / MICHAEL CAPUTO, Residence Halls / ARLENE CARDEN, Vice President of Planning Office / ANNETTE CARROLL, Treasurer's Office / ROSE CAVANAUGH, Nurse / MARGARET CICERINI, Estate / THOMAS CLARK,

Residence Halls / MARILYN COAR, President's Office / BETTY CONNOR, Cafeteria / GERALD CONNORS, Long Center / PAUL CONLON, Long Center / ROBERT DEFAZIO JR., Cafeteria / FRANK DEPIETRO, Cafeteria / THOMAS DEPIETRO, Cafeteria / FRANK DOHERTY, St. Thomas Hall / ROBERT DOHERTY, Student Center / MARY DONLY, Estate / KATHLEEN DUNLEAVY, Registrar's Office / DORIS EDSELL, Data Processing / JANE EMERY, Placement Office / MARTHA EVANS, Cafeteria / MARY FARRELL, PBX / JAMES FABRELL, Print Shop / LOUISE FEITERGE, Faculty Office / LAWSON FOICE, St. Thomas Hall / DOLORES FOIKIN, Registrar's Office / ROSEMARY FOX, Treasurer's Office / JESSI FURTINI, Residence Halls / EDWARD GALLAGHER, Residence

Windhover Yearbook
University of Scranton
1972

Unsung Pillars of the University of Scranton

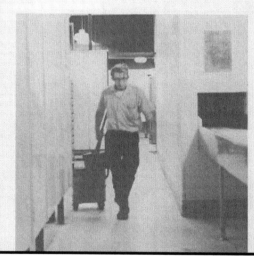

STANLEY LANKOWSKI, Library / ALMA LEWIS, Cafeteria / KATHERINE LOPATKA, Cafeteria / MRS. ALICE LOUGHMAN, Cafeteria / ALICE LOUGHMAN, Cafeteria / JAMES MACK, Print Shop / CATHERINE MALIA, Treasurer's Office / EUGENE MAHONEY, Loyola Hall / GLYNN MARTINO, Print Shop / JOHN MASLANY, Student Center / AGNES MAYER, Residence Halls / JOHN McCRONE, Student Center / DALE McELROY, Athletics / MARY McGLOIN, Cafeteria / CYNTHIA McKNIGHT, Registrar's Office / ROSE MECCA, Residence Halls / JOSEPH METZGER, Cafeteria / JOSEPH MICHALIK, St. Thomas Hall / HAROLD MILES, Long Center / GRACE MILLER, Advanced Study Advisory Office / ESTELLE MISOREK, Computer Center / MARY MITCHELL, Residence Halls / DONNA MOFFITT, Bookstore / JOSEPH MOFFITT, Long Center / JOSEPH MORENO, Cafeteria / ALICE MURPHY, Registrar's Office / JAMES MURPHY, Painter / MARGARET MURRIN, Dean of Arts and Sciences Office / RANDOLPH MYERS, Library / ROBERT NEALIS, Bookstore / SANDRA NITCH, Education Dept. / SHARON NOLAN, Treasurer's Office / CARYL NOTCHICK, Business Dept. / ANTHONY NOTO, Residence Halls / ALEX OBIODINSKI, Groundsman / ARLENE OLIVETTI, Library / GEORGE ONOFREY, Cafeteria / ROSE ORLANDO, Cafeteria / BENNY PAMBIANCO, Cafeteria / CHIARA PERSICHETTI, Library / DOLORES PISARSKI, Admissions Office / MARIANNE PIRINO, Student Personnel Office / JULIA POLLACK, Residence Halls / ALFONSO RANIELLA, Estate / TONY REDINSKI, Cafeteria / JOSEPH REILLY, Loyola Hall / MARY ANN RESARIK, Research Bureau / MICHAEL RINCAVAGE, Residence Halls / HELEN RINDILLA, Estate / MARY ANN RIEBE, Computer Center / MARTHA ROSPIG, LEOS, Student Personnel Office / MARY RYAN, Counseling Center / CERI RYBTSKI, Cafeteria / JEAN SCRIMIERI, Cafeteria / BETTY SCHOLLA, Treasurer's Office / DONNA SCOFICHAS, Library / FRANK SHLTKUPSKI, Maintenance Supervisor / WILLIAM SHLTKUPSKI, Carpenter / STEPHANIE SILVESTRI, Graduate Office / MICHAEL SIZE, Cafeteria / ELAINE SKEREROY, Alumni Office / ANTHONY SNOLESKI, Painter / JACOB SNYDER, St. Thomas Hall / RUTH SNYDER, Treasurer's Office / MARY SPELLMAN, Residence Halls / BARBARA SPENCER, Faculty Offices / JAMES TALERICO, Estate / STANLEY TAVERNI, Cafeteria / MARY TERRINONE, Language Laboratory / ALFRED THOMAS, Student Center / LILLIAN THOMPSON, Administrative Offices / CARMELLA VERDETTO, Residence Halls / JOAN VOCHNSKY, PBX / PETER WALSH, St. Thomas Hall / THOMAS WALSH, Estate / ISABELLE WILLIAMS, Bursar / LOUISE WISION, Graduate Office / JUDY VOCTANIS, Cafeteria

Windhover Yearbook
University of Scranton
1972

Chapter Three

Memories and Milestones: The 1972 Staff at the University of Scranton

Unsung Pillars of the University of Scranton

The 1972 'Windhover' yearbook produced by the University of Scranton is more than a mere annual publication; it is a historical document providing the only complete publicly available record of the University's employees from that era.

Notably, it recognizes senior management and chronicles the line employees—the true bedrock of the institution. Line employees, or administrative staff, refer to the individuals directly involved in the University's day-to-day operations and administrative tasks. These employees play a crucial role in the smooth running of the institution, often working behind the scenes in various departments to ensure efficiency and effectiveness in the University's operations.

By assiduously gathering data from multiple resources, including genealogical websites, local newspapers, public records, and university archives, the compilers crafted a detailed alphabetical list of 151 administrative and support staff, each accompanied by their departmental roles. Now transformed into concise biographical vignettes, this project honors the dedicated service of these individuals, allowing readers to appreciate the foundational figures who contribute tirelessly to uphold the University's standard of excellence.

Unsung Pillars of the University of Scranton

3.1 Abbey Abbott
Library

Abbey Abbott's life was a Scranton story, through and through. Born to the late Nardellis, she carried the city in her bones, walking its streets, breathing its air. A West Side Central Catholic and Lackawanna Junior College grad, she later juggled the ledgers at Scranton Bank, paced the precincts at the Police Department, and filed for Peters Associates.

But her real work? Volunteering at the Heart Association, campaigning for life, praying at St. Ann's, where the Maronite bells tolled for the faith she held dear. Abbey swam, crafted, and puzzled out phrases on 'Wheel of Fortune—a local champ in her own right. Sundays were sacred, spent around family tables, her nieces' and nephews' laughter seasoning the air. Friends spoke of her sincerity, her heart.

Abbey, who passed away in the early 2000s, lived a simple, devout, faithful Scranton life.

3.2 Gary Ackerman
Treasurer's Office

Gary Ackerman's life is a narrative of unwavering commitment to service and continuous self-improvement. He graduated from Central High School in 1965 and promptly enlisted in the Air Force, where he quickly stood out at Sheppard Air Force Base in Texas, earning the title "Airman of the Month." His dedication to service was matched by a romantic chapter that began with courtship and led to marriage in 1967, followed by life in France and England.

During his time overseas, Ackerman diligently pursued his education through the University of Maryland Extension School, a global program allowing military personnel and others to study while stationed abroad. After returning to the United States, he continued his studies in evening classes while working by day. His dedication culminated in a Bachelor of Science in Business Administration by 1973.

Simultaneously, Ackerman's career progressed in the treasurer's office, where he showcased his skill in finance. His life exemplifies an extraordinary balance between professional development, academic achievement, and personal life, reflecting a deep commitment to his country and himself.

3.3 Gerald Allen
Student Center

In the 1970s, Gerald Allen was one of many staff members who maintained the University's spirit. His work at the student center, a vibrant heart of dreams and learning, was crucial for its smooth running, though his name didn't make it into history books.

The staff, a diverse group of unrecognized individuals, played a unique yet connected role. They were keepers of the University's traditions and forward movement, safeguarding and advancing the University's heritage year by year. Gerald was a part of this silent pledge.

Their impact exceeded their job roles; they fostered an atmosphere conducive to learning and growth. Their quiet contributions were vital in providing a supportive environment for students' educational paths.

Gerald's contributions were essential, though not singularly celebrated. Alongside his peers, he was an integral part of the University's community, helping to uphold a culture of hard work, teamwork, and a profound dedication to academic excellence.

Unsung Pillars of the University of Scranton

3.4 Patsy Amori
Estate

Patsy Amori dedicated his life to service, evidenced by his well-worn hands that resembled an aged cutting board. He spent his days in the Jesuit estate's kitchen, which was much more than a mere workspace to him. It was a sacred space where the cooking scents mingled with the spirit of prayer.

Amori's early years were shaped by war, serving twice (World War II and Korea) and reaching the rank of Sergeant First Class. The discipline he learned in the military was evident in his approach to cooking. In the 1970s, at a Catholic university, he crafted meals that spoke of faith and simplicity. He used local ingredients, and his menus celebrated the changing seasons and observed Lent.

His wife, Matilda, saw beyond the chef's apron to the man inside, a self-taught cook whose talent surpassed many formally trained chefs. Although he never earned a diploma, Amori's contribution was recognized by the Order of Pro Deo et Universitate, an honor that survived him. He was a humble man who nourished many, and he rests in Scranton's Cathedral Cemetery, a part of the city's rich history.

Unsung Pillars of the University of Scranton

Born in 1917, Amori passed away in 1976. Although his life's flame has been extinguished, the warmth and comfort he provided through his cooking continue to be felt.

Unsung Pillars of the University of Scranton

3.5 Michael Balendy
Residence Halls

Michael Balendy's life story is deeply rooted in Scranton, Pennsylvania, where he was laid to rest in 1979. A proud World War II veteran, he served with honor as a Fireman First Class in the U.S. Navy, which speaks volumes of his enduring commitment to service. After the war, he anchored his life in the familiar streets of Scranton, marrying Gertrude Bruno in 1944. Their home was a bustling hive of activity, with the laughter and footsteps of their six sons and five daughters.

In the 1970s, Balendy's dedication shone through in his work at the University of Scranton. As a maintenance employee, he was the unseen hand, ensuring the campus was a well-oiled machine. The University of Scranton, guided by Jesuit principles that advocate for education, social justice, and helping others, provided a backdrop for Balendy's work. A Jesuit institution is managed by the Society of Jesus, a Catholic order known for its commitment to rigorous education and its students' moral and spiritual enrichment. Balendy's role in maintaining the University's buildings and grounds was more than mere upkeep; it was a manifestation of excellence and service.

In those times, technology was not as advanced as today, and Balendy's tasks required a hands-on approach relying on manual relational tools. Whether it was fixing a leaky faucet or setting up for a campus event, his work was a tangible expression of the Jesuit ethos, which emphasizes respect for the environment, community involvement, and a dedication to the collective mission of the University.

Balendy's life in Scranton extended beyond the University. He was a member of Saint Peter's Cathedral, bringing the same dedication to his faith community as he did to his professional role. His story, from the seas of World War II to the serene corridors of the University of Scranton, is a testament to service, family, and faith. Buried in Scranton, his legacy is interwoven with the city's very essence and adherence to the values he held dear.

3.6 Kathleen Barrett
Computer Center

Kathleen Barrett, a steadfast figure of Scranton, PA, wove the fabric of her life tightly with the threads of family, faith, and the fledgling field of computers. Born to Francis and Sara Kearney Barrett, she navigated the world alongside two brothers and three sisters, only to return to the roots of her cherished hometown at the close of her earthly chapter in 2015 at the tender age of 80.

Her life was a tapestry of dedication—34 years spent as a computer operator at the University of Scranton, a tenure that spanned the infancy of modern computing. In the days when mainframes ruled, and computers hummed with the collective workload of batch jobs and punch cards, Kathleen was the sentinel at the gates of this burgeoning digital cosmos. The era in which Kathleen worked was transformative, bridging the mechanical and the digital, with computing machines evolving from room-sized mainframes operated by punch cards to the advent of personal computing.

Amidst this technological revolution, Kathleen's role as a female computer operator was both a rarity and a statement of pioneering resilience. At a time when male achievements predominately narrated the field, she supported the University's academic mission and carved a path for future women in technology. Her expertise in managing the lifeblood of the University's computing needs—from the whir of tape drives to the clatter of printers and the meticulous data entry that built the backbone of academic records—was instrumental and revolutionary.

A South Catholic High School graduate and a lifelong St. Joseph's Church member at Divine Mercy Parish, Kathleen's faith was as integral to her as her work. She was a presence at the Divine Mercy Table, a testament to her spirit of giving and community. The University of Scranton recognized her service with the Order Pro Deo Et Universitate—an honor mirroring her commitment to God and education. Yet, the simple, unquantifiable moments with family and friends brought her the purest joy, a sentiment felt deeply by those who knew her love.

Kathleen's passing left a void in the hearts of many, marked by the absence of her siblings, Mary Frances Ryan, Margaret Skoda, and Thomas Barrett. Her life, stitched with the love of her family and the advances of her time, remains a narrative of a woman steadfast in her contributions to the evolving world and her community. Her story is not just one of personal perseverance but also of women's silent yet significant contributions to the technological tapestry that defines our modern era.

3.7 Margaret Bass
Residence Halls

In 1972, within the bustling campus of the University of Scranton, there was a figure whose presence, though quiet and unassuming, was a constant in the ever-changing tapestry of college life. This was Margaret Bass, her name a solitary entry on an employee list, her exact role shrouded in the folds of time. With no precise details of her duties, we delve into a respectful and plausible imagining of her day, a tribute to the many unsung individuals who shape our shared spaces.

Margaret Bass: Unveiling Campus Life at the University of Scranton, 1972

As dawn's light touched the University of Scranton, Margaret Bass began her day amidst the historical architecture and vibrant student life. Her undefined yet integral role found her moving through the campus with a quiet purpose.

Margaret's day might have been filled with various tasks, each contributing to the smooth running of the University. Perhaps she was part of the administrative staff, her fingers dancing over a typewriter, transcribing notes and memos that kept the academic gears turning. Or maybe she found herself in the

Unsung Pillars of the University of Scranton

library amidst rows of books, ensuring that knowledge was neatly shelved and readily accessible to curious minds.

Her interaction with students could have been fleeting yet meaningful – a reassuring smile here, a gentle word of encouragement there. She might have been a familiar presence in the bustling cafeteria, overseeing the daily dance of meal preparations and service, ensuring no student went hungry.

Lunchtime would be a simple affair, often shared with colleagues whose stories and laughter brought warmth to any ordinary day. The afternoon might usher in more responsibilities - perhaps attending to administrative duties, assisting in event preparations, or even tending to the verdant campus grounds.

As the day unfolded, Margaret might have paused to observe the ebb and flow of campus life – the youthful exuberance, the scholarly debates, and the quiet moments of introspection. Though not clearly defined, her role was a thread in this academic community's fabric.

Evening's approach signaled the end of her workday. She would leave the campus, her contributions for the day unseen but vital, her presence a subtle yet enduring part of the University's rhythm.

Margaret Bass, a name from a past era, represents the myriad of individuals whose roles in educational institutions, often unnoticed, are essential cogs in the wheel of academic and community life. Her story, woven from the threads of imagination, pays homage to those who contribute in countless, often unacknowledged, ways to our collective experience in such vibrant communal spaces.

3.8 Lloyd Beam
Long Center

The story of Lloyd Franklin Beam is an essential piece of Northeastern Pennsylvania's history. Born in the coal mining town of Hazleton in 1928, Lloyd's journey reflects the shift from the gritty life of coal mining to the bustling world of college athletics. Although there's no official record of his role at the University of Scranton's Long Center, local lore suggests that he was part of the team there in 1972.

Lloyd may have been responsible for the upkeep and organization of sports events at the University, making sure everything from the condition of the courts and fields to the availability of sports gear was in top shape for every game. His work was more than just maintenance; it was about ensuring the University's values and traditions were upheld in every match and practice session.

His life was a testament to dedication: he was a family man, married with a daughter, and his career transition from the coal mines to a potential position at a college sports facility marked a personal evolution when college sports became a major cultural force.

Unsung Pillars of the University of Scranton

We may never have official documentation of Lloyd's time at the University, but what remains is a powerful narrative of a man whose life's work, though not recorded in written form, lives on through the stories told by those who remember him. His legacy mirrors the enduring character of the region, from his birth in 1928 to his passing in 2007. Lloyd Franklin Beam's life story, validated by those who knew him rather than by paper trails, continues to resonate as a tribute to the hardworking spirit of Northeastern Pennsylvania.

3.9 Rita Bellas
Cafeteria

Rita Bellas was a cherished figure at the University of Scranton, where her warm presence graced the cafeteria for four decades. Serving through the heart of the mid-20th century, she became a familiar face to generations of students, offering nourishment and a touch of maternal care.

A Dunmore High School graduate, Rita's days were filled with the grill sizzle and the trays clatter as she juggled cooking homestyle meals, managing inventory, and ensuring the dining hall's cleanliness. Her role extended beyond mere food preparation; she was an unsung hero of the university community, her smile steady in the bustling campus life.

In 1987, Rita's dedication was recognized with the Pro Deo et Universitate Award, a testament to her service, which mirrored the institution's ethos. Her commitment wasn't limited to the university boundaries; in 1967, Rita took on a vital role in the Cancer Crusade, showcasing her spirit of community activism.

At home in Dunmore, PA, Rita was the heart of her household and a beloved wife and mother to three daughters. She relished sitting on her porch, where laughter and stories with family and friends were as plentiful as the servings she dished out.

Unsung Pillars of the University of Scranton

Rita's legacy, marked by the year of her passing in 2010, remains etched in the memories of those who knew her, a beacon of the community spirit and personal touch that seems so rare in today's fast-paced world.

3.10 Judith Black
Financial Aid

In the quaint corridors of the University of Scranton's Financial Aid Office, Judith Black was a name etched on a roster, lingering in the annals of 1972. With no definitive information to color her days, we can only imagine her world, filled with the hum of calculators and the rustle of paper applications.

The era cast a unique hue on her role; this was when financial aid was a labyrinth of manual processes, where ledgers and forms were the maps and compasses. Judith's days were likely spent in the diligent review of applications, her eyes scanning the fine print, deciphering the needs and aspirations of the students before her.

She may have been the bridge between policy and possibility, her advice sowing the seeds of opportunity in a garden of economic uncertainty. In an office where each file held a different dream, Judith's task would have been to navigate the delicate balance of budgets and benevolence, her decisions quietly sculpting the future.

At a Catholic university, her work was perhaps touched by the institution's ethos, where the values of community and stewardship whispered through the halls. Here, Judith would

Unsung Pillars of the University of Scranton

stand as a guardian of potential, ensuring that financial constraints did not deter the pursuit of knowledge.

Though the specifics of Judith Black's character and practices remain unknown, her role in the fabric of the University of Scranton was undoubtedly pivotal. In every line of data, in every awarded grant or scholarship, her unseen hand played a part in crafting the narrative of countless graduates. In this way, through the legacy of her position, Judith Black comes alive—a silent protagonist in the University's enduring story.

Unsung Pillars of the University of Scranton

3.11 Frank Bloom
Cafeteria

Frank Bloom was a man of routine, the kind that studs a university's heart with the permanence of its bricks. In '72, he stood behind the counters of the University of Scranton's cafeteria, donning a white apron that seemed to bear the stains of a thousand meals like badges of honor. To students, he was a fixture as familiar as the chapel bell, dishing out comfort through hot meals and a stern nod.

He wasn't the sort to wax poetic about his work. Frank saw his job in simple terms: serve the food, keep the line moving, maintain cleanliness, and ensure no student went hungry. His hands, weathered and steady, were adept at juggling tasks, from operating the cash register to mopping up spills.

His ethic was blue-collar, hewn from a belief in the dignity of labor. The cafeteria hummed under his watch, each tray a testament to his quiet dedication. He didn't need the limelight; satisfaction came in the rhythm of daily toil, the clatter of dishes, and the ebb and flow of youthful chatter.

Did he find it fulfilling? That was a question for folks with the luxury of choice. For Frank, fulfillment was in the doing, the providing, and the everyday giving. In the grand tapestry of university life, he was a single, steadfast thread, holding his small corner with unwavering certainty. Frank Bloom, the unsung steward of sustenance, embodied the spirit of an era where work was its reward.

3.12 George Bodnar
Mail Room

In a corner office, huddled among stacks of letters and parcels, sat George Bodnar, a sentinel of the written word in an era unfathomed by today's digital natives. George's story, a tapestry of diligent service woven into the very fabric of the University, is one of quiet significance, a testament to the roles often overlooked yet indispensable.

Born in the cradle of 1913 to parents cradling dreams of a better life across the ocean from Austria-Hungary, George's life was a mosaic of the American experience. A graduate in chemistry in 1936, he was the alchemist of the University's communications, transmuting the mundane task of mail distribution into the gold thread that held the institution together.

For 37 years, his office was a hub, a pulsating heart through which the lifeblood of information flowed. To say George was responsible for mail is to say the sky is responsible for blue. It was a dance of envelopes and packages; each step choreographed with precision, a ballet of balance between confidentiality and urgency.

George's commitment echoed the times of his youth, where responsibility was not just a word but a creed. The values of hard

Unsung Pillars of the University of Scranton

work and reliability were forged in the clatter of the textile factory where he first worked. These values he brought to the University, where his office became a beacon, a lighthouse guiding the institutional ships through the fog of daily operations.

His life was not all letters and stamps, though. In 1934, as the leading scorer of his parish basketball team and later in the YMCA league, George dribbled and shot his way into the hearts of his community. By 1950, he took to the sidelines, not to rest, but to serve as the trainer for the University football team, his hands now mending muscles and spirits.

The Pro Deo et Universitate award found its way to him in 1974, an emblem of his unwavering service, a recognition that perhaps shone a light too bright on a man accustomed to the shadows of duty. In life, he was celebrated quietly, and in death, the president of the University, an institution he served with the steadfastness of a sentinel, observed mass at his funeral.

George Bodnar's story is not of rags to riches nor heroic feats in the eyes of the world. His was a life of steadfast commitment, a chapter in the book of the University that may not be turned to often but whose words are imprinted deeply in its history. His final rest is in Saint Mary's Greek Catholic Cemetery in the Minooka section. Still, a geographical marker for his legacy lies within the University's corridors, in the fluttering of every letter delivered, in every student and staff whose day ran smoother because of his silent vigil.

As readers, we may not find our lives mirrored in George's, but we can find inspiration. For within his story lies a universal truth – that every role, no matter how seemingly small, has its place in the larger narrative, and every life, lived with purpose and dedication, is a story worth telling.

Unsung Pillars of the University of Scranton

Unsung Pillars of the University of Scranton

3.13 Jeanne Brack
Print Shop

In the heart of Scranton, amidst the burgeoning spirit of the early 1970s, stood the University of Scranton print shop—a humming nexus where academia met the press. Amidst the rhythmic lull of machinery, Jeanne Brack found her calling. In a time when higher education was still blossoming in the embrace of the Catholic tradition, Jeanne's role in the print shop was pivotal. She was the unseen hand that crafted the materials that shaped minds, the artisan of the printed word that threaded through the campus.

Jeanne's days were spent amidst stacks of paper, the scent of fresh ink, and the clamor of machines. Her duties were manifold; she might have been setting type, aligning plates, or binding theses. The print shop was an essential cog in the University's wheel, producing academic journals, lecture notes, and perhaps even the campus newspaper. Each sheet passed through her hands was a testament to the educational journey of countless students.

Graduating cum laude from Lackawanna Junior College in 1979, Jeanne's academic journey was both a personal triumph and a beacon of inspiration. It was a feat that did not go unnoticed, as the local newspaper extolled her dedication, highlighting her role as vice president of student government for the weekend/evening division—a clear sign of her leadership and commitment to her peers.

Unsung Pillars of the University of Scranton

Born in 1930, Jeanne's roots ran deep in Scranton's soil. A proud West Scranton High School graduate, she carried the essence of the city within her. Her professional life was marked by years of meticulous service as a bookkeeper for the Scranton Electric Construction company, a testament to her precision and integrity.

Faith was a cornerstone of Jeanne's life, with Saint Patrick's Church in West Scranton symbolizing her spiritual devotion. Her faith was a quiet strength underpinning her journey as a widow and a mother to several sons through moments of joy and times of trial.

Jeanne's story is not just one of personal achievement and steadfast work ethic but also of the profound impact of the mundane, often overlooked tasks that keep the wheels of institutions turning. Her legacy is etched not only in the annals of the University of Scranton print shop but also in the hearts of her family, friends, and all those who walked the halls of academia that her hands helped sustain.

Jeanne Brack, a daughter of Scranton, passed away in 2003 in the same city that shaped her life's narrative—a narrative rich with diligence, learning, and an unwavering spirit reflective of the era she lived in and the community she served.

Unsung Pillars of the University of Scranton

3.14 James Brown
Bookstore

In the early 1970s, at the heart of the University of Scranton, the campus bookstore stood as a bustling hub, integral to the academic and social life of the institution. Here, we find James Brown, listed in the 1972 yearbook, whose role in this vibrant space is left mainly to the imagination, with no further details to sketch out the lines of his life.

Picture the university bookstore during this era: a place where knowledge was not just sold but shared, where textbooks and literature lined the shelves, inviting young minds to explore worlds beyond their classrooms. Like James, the employees of such a place would have been the custodians of this gateway to knowledge. Their responsibilities, while primarily centered around the logistics of managing a bookstore - from stocking shelves to handling transactions - also placed them at the intersection of academic life and personal growth for the students.

These bookstore employees, often unnoticed, played a silent yet significant role in the educational journey of many. They provided the tools - the books, the materials, the resources - that fueled the intellectual curiosity of a generation poised on the brink of change. A thirst marked the era for learning and understanding the world in new and challenging ways.

The bookstore was more than a commercial space; it was communal. It was where students congregated, discussed, debated, and ideas were as much a commodity as the books lined the shelves. While not directly involved in the educational process, employees in such a setting facilitated it in their own way. They ensured that students had access to the required texts, and often, they were the ones who witnessed the frantic last-minute rush before exams or the eager search for a much-needed reference book.

James Brown, as an employee of this bookstore, would have been part of this dynamic environment. While not detailed in the annals of history, his role was nonetheless a part of the tapestry of university life. The bookstore, under the stewardship of its employees, was a space where knowledge was accessible, where learning was supported, and where the academic journey found one of its many starting points.

While we know little about James Brown's personal story or his impact as an individual, his role in the University of Scranton's bookstore positions him within a narrative of quiet contribution to the academic and personal growth of those who passed through its doors. In this way, his presence, though undetailed, remains a small yet integral part of the University's history.

3.15 Edward Buchalski (Junior)
Residence Halls

In the early 1970s, Edward's world was the halls of the University of Scranton, where the hum of his maintenance cart was a familiar refrain. With a tool belt clasped around his waist, he was a silent sentinel of the student's home away from home. His days were spent in the cyclical rhythm of repairs, upkeep, and the occasional lifesaving intervention when students locked themselves out before finals. Edward knew the pulse of the place—the clang of the heating pipes, the flicker of a bulb on the brink—and he tended to it all with a craftsman's care.

Maintenance work is often invisible, yet the linchpin holds the community's day-to-day life together. Edward was a keeper of this unseen order, a steward of the mundane yet essential tasks that make a residence hall home. Cleaning, fixing, replacing—these were the verbs of his working life, performed with a meticulousness born of a deep-seated respect for the institution and its inhabitants.

The Young Adult Golden Age Club knew Edward for his stories and his silent, knowing smiles. They would gather, a congregation of shared memories, where Edward's presence was a gentle reminder of the beauty in routine and the dignity of labor.

His final rest came in 2006, beneath the soil of Sacred Hearts Cemetery in Minooka, where the echoes of a life lived in simple service lies with him. Edward Buchalski, a man of Scranton, whose legacy is etched not in stone but in the countless lives eased by his toil, reminds us that life need not be loud to be monumental. His was a melody of maintenance; a life lived in the key of devotion.

3.16 James Burns
Cafeteria

In a tribute to everyday heroes, James J. Burns stands out—a man whose legacy is warmly remembered by those who walked the halls of the University of Scranton. Born in 1936, James, known to many as Jim, dedicated over thirty years to the University, not as a faculty member but as the director of dining services through a contractor named Aramark.

Imagine Jim in the bustling era of the 1970s, a time of social change and academic exploration. He was more than just the dining hall manager; he was a figure of stability and generosity. Daily, he ensured that the 600 students who used the dining facilities received food and a sense of home. Jim's introduction of "Unlimited seconds"—meaning students could return for as much food as they wanted at breakfast and dinner—was a revolutionary idea then. It wasn't just about providing more food but ensuring no student left the dining hall hungry.

Jim's journey with education began long before his time at Scranton. He was a proud Altoona Catholic High School and Pennsylvania State University graduate. His move to Scranton in 1965 to take up a position at the University was the start of an impactful career. He wasn't just overseeing the operation of serving meals; he was nurturing a community, making the dining hall a place where students felt supported.

His passion for sports, perhaps reflective of his belief in teamwork and community, was a well-known aspect of his character. He brought the same enthusiasm to his role as President of the Northeastern Pennsylvania Restaurant Association, representing local eateries and advocating for their interests.

Jim's commitment to service was recognized when he was inducted into the Order of Pro Deo et Universitate. This was a rare honor, especially since he was technically not a university employee, highlighting how integral he was to the University's community. In memory of his service, the James Burns Memorial Scholarship was established, providing financial support to students, a lasting tribute to his belief in the value of education.

In 1998, Burns was named the Greater Scranton Penn State Alumnus of the Year, a fitting accolade for someone who always held his alma mater close to his heart.

A family man, Jim's legacy lives on not just through the scholarship bearing his name or the honors he received but in the lives of his family members and the students whose college experience he enriched. Jim passed away in 2006, but the principles he embodied—generosity, service, and community—continue to inspire those who remember him at the University of Scranton.

3.17 Rosemary Butler
Evening College

In the heart of Scranton, where the pulse of academia beats within the venerable walls of the University of Scranton, there walked an indispensable and understated figure—Rosemary Butler. Born in 1924 to a family woven into the city's tapestry, with a father at the helm of a local business beacon, Rosemary was a thread in the community's fabric, her life a tapestry of service and dedication.

Graduating from Central High School amidst the echoes of a world at war in 1941, she carried the spirit of her hometown into her studies at Marywood College, emerging with a Bachelor of Science degree in 1945. It was the same year she stepped into the corridors of power, serving as a secretary to the Bureau of Aeronautics at the U.S. Navy Department in Washington, D.C. Her journey there was a prelude to a pivotal role at Eastman Kodak, where she honed her skills as an executive assistant until 1964.

Her return to Scranton was a homecoming to her roots and to a role that would define her legacy. As secretary to the Dean of the Evening College at the University of Scranton, Rosemary was the ligament that connected the students and faculty, her responsibilities extending far beyond the typed letter and the managed schedule. She was the unseen hand guiding the college's day-to-day life, a steward of education's silent hours.

Her brother, Reverend Henry J. Butler, SJ, found his calling within the same hallowed halls, serving in a senior position. Together, they represented a family legacy of faith and education, their paths intertwined with the institution's destiny.

Rosemary's service was a beacon that burned steadily through decades, and she was recognized in 1984 with the Pro Deo Et Universitate award—an accolade honoring her unwavering commitment. She had seen the University's landscape change as she assisted Assistant to the Dean of Dexter Hanley College in 1979, her expertise and wisdom shaping the institution's growth.

Her affiliations with the Marywood College Alumnae Association, Cross Keys Fraternity, and the University of Scranton Clerical Association were not mere titles but extensions of her community spirit, her belief in the power of connection, and education.

When Rosemary passed away in 2005 at 81, she left behind more than just memories. She left a legacy etched into the very soul of Scranton, a testament to a life of service. A life lived with quiet dignity and unspoken heroism—the epitome of what it means to be a community pillar.

Unsung Pillars of the University of Scranton

3.18 Michael Caputo
Residence Halls

Michael Caputo's story, a figure from the early 1970s at the University of Scranton, is one woven from the threads of imagination and respect, pieced together from the scant detail of his name on a list, indicating his role in serving the residence halls. In envisioning his life, we tread the line between fact and fiction, aiming to honor his contribution without overstating the known.

In those years, the University of Scranton was a bustling hub, alive with the energy of students carving out their paths in the world. Michael, likely part of the maintenance staff, played a crucial yet often overlooked role in this vibrant community. His days may have been spent in the background, ensuring the smooth running of the residence halls, which were more than just buildings. They were homes away from home, where friendships were forged and young minds nurtured.

Imagine Michael moving through the halls, a familiar and reassuring presence. His often-unseen work was essential in creating an environment where students could live and learn without worrying about the physical space around them. In fixing a broken window, tending to heat issues, or ensuring the lights worked, Michael contributed to a sense of safety and comfort, vital for any learning environment.

His impact, though subtle, was profound. Academics and extracurriculars do not just shape the ethos of a university, but also the sense of community and well-being fostered within its walls. Michael, through his dedication to maintaining the residence halls, played a part in promoting this. His work helped create a space where students could focus on their studies and personal growth, free from the distractions of a less cared-for living environment.

Michael's story, though largely unknown, is a reminder of the countless individuals who contribute in significant yet unrecognized ways to the growth and development of educational institutions. His role at the University of Scranton, while not documented in detail, was undoubtedly vital in its day-to-day life and in shaping its ethos of care, community, and support.

In celebrating Michael Caputo, we celebrate all those who work behind the scenes, whose names may not be widely known but whose contributions are the bedrock upon which institutions stand. His legacy, though not recorded in history books, lives on in the spirit of the University of Scranton and in the appreciation for those who dedicate themselves to the betterment of such communities.

Unsung Pillars of the University of Scranton

3.19 Arlene Carden
Vice President of Planning Office

Arlene Carden's story is etched in the annals of Scranton's modest history, not through grandiose deeds but through the steadfast rhythm of her daily toil. Born in the winter of 1918, her narrative began in the shadow of a world at war, a preamble that perhaps lent a certain resilience to her character.

In the hallowed halls of the Technical High School, young Arlene's mind was sharpened, a prelude to the further honing it would receive at the Powell School of Business. These institutions, foundational in her journey, were the forges where her capability and resolve were tempered.

Upon her graduation, the wheels of fate saw her through the doors of the General Mills Corporation. It was here, amid the hum of industry, that Arlene cut her teeth in the professional world. But as the tides of time ebbed and flowed, so did the chapters of her career.

By 1972, Arlene found herself in the corridors of academia, serving as a secretary to an executive at the University of Scranton. Her role was one of silent significance, a custodian of the meticulous planning that underpins the educational edifice. She was the unsung architect of schedules, the weaver of administrative threads, and the keeper of confidential dialogues. Her days were a tapestry of appointments, correspondence, and the occasional soothing of academic egos. She was the discreet sentinel at the gate of innovation and progress, ensuring the machinery of the University's future was well-oiled and directed.

Outside the demands of her profession, Arlene's heart found solace and purpose in the Hickory Street Presbyterian Church. Her faith was a quiet flame that warmed her through the trials of life, including the loss of her spouse, leaving her a widow in a world that often overlooked the silent sufferings of such solitary figures.

She was interwoven into the community fabric through her involvement with the Women of Hickory and the Order of the Eastern Star. Here, she was not just Arlene the professional but Arlene the friend, the confidant, the sister in arms. These affiliations were her outreach, her way of imprinting on the world around her, leaving whispers of her presence in charitable works and shared moments of fellowship.

When 1994 drew the curtains on her earthly presence, Arlene left behind a legacy not etched in stone but carried in the hearts of those she touched. Scranton held on to her memory, enshrining her within its verdant embrace, where she was laid to rest.
Whippernock

Arlene's story is not one of the loud triumphs but of quiet constancy—a testament to the uncelebrated but essential threads that hold the fabric of society together. Her life, a narrative of dedication, faith, and resilience, resonates in the silent spaces of Scranton's memory, as enduring as the city's storied hills.

Unsung Pillars of the University of Scranton

3.20 Annette Carroll
Treasurer's Office

In Scranton's heart was a woman of modest means and rich spirit, Annette Carroll by name, whose days were woven into the fabric of the University of Scranton's Treasurer's Office. In the era of rotary phones and typewriters clacking like a metronome dictating the pace of work, Annette found her rhythm. The office, a symphony of ledger books and carbon copies, was her domain from '72 until her retirement in '82. In those days, calculators were as close to computers as they got, and meticulousness was not a virtue but a necessity.

With a pencil tucked in her hair, Annette became a fixture at the University, as much a part of it as the bricks and mortar of the buildings themselves. The technology of the time required a deft hand and an even steadier mind, qualities Annette possessed in abundance. Numbers were her notes, and she played them with the precision of a maestro, ensuring that every tuition payment and expenditure was accounted for down to the last penny.

A life-long resident of Scranton, Annette's roots ran as deep as the coal mines that once defined the city. A widow for many years, she had known love that lasted over half a century, a testament to her steadfast nature. Her faith was as much a part of her as her blue-collar work ethic, and the Nativity of Our Lord church saw her every Sunday without fail, her voice a soft harmony in the choir of the faithful.

Outside the meticulous world of figures and finances, Annette found solace in life's simple joys. Her garden was a tapestry of colors, a place of tranquility where she would lose herself among the blossoms, with the serene company of chirping birds. Family gatherings were her highlight, her home an open heart where laughter was served generously alongside her home-cooked meals.

Annette's journey ended in the same town where it began, in the embrace of the valley that had shaped her. She departed in 2010, leaving the legacy of a life rooted in community, faith, and the simple pleasures that stitch the days together. She rests now in Cathedral Cemetery, under the same sky she watched with wonder, the birds she adored now singing for her.

Unsung Pillars of the University of Scranton

Unsung Pillars of the University of Scranton

3.21 Rose Cavanaugh
Nurse

In the rhythmic cadence of everyday voices, let us weave the story of Rose Cavanaugh, a beacon of care and compassion in the University of Scranton community.

Rose, with the steadfast spirit of her hometown, carried the legacy of the hardworking Pennsylvania coal country in her bones. A graduate of Throop High School, she had the tenacity and grit emblematic of her era, traits that propelled her from defense production in New Jersey to the honorable ranks of the U.S. Navy. As a pharmacist mate in the Hospital Corps, Rose exemplified the service and sacrifice of the Greatest Generation.

Upon returning to Scranton, her calling in nursing found a new home at Mercy Hospital. There, she didn't just dispense medicine but also dispensed wisdom, serving as both supervisor and clinical instructor. Her knowledge was a gift she gave freely, nurturing the next generation of nurses with a blend of discipline and kindness.

But it was at the University of Scranton that Rose's legacy took root. In partnership with the university administration, she founded the first infirmary—a haven where young scholars, away from home and needing care, found a guardian. As the chief architect of this sanctuary of health, Rose was more than a nurse; she was a confidante, a counselor, and a surrogate mother to many. Her daily duties spanned the gamut from treating the flu to mending broken spirits, each task performed with an unwavering dedication to her charges.

A devout woman, Rose's faith was as integral to her being as her nursing cap. Her daily attendance at mass was a testament to her deep faith, which spilled into her volunteer work with the Church of the Nativity of Our Lord. Her hands, skilled in healing, were equally adept at service, whether through the Mercy Hospital Alumni Society or the various church societies, she bolstered with her leadership.

Rose's love story with her husband spanned over five decades, a testament to her capacity for deep, abiding affection. Her life, stitched together with devotion to her family and community, was a tapestry of service.

In 2005, Rose passed away, leaving behind a legacy as enduring as the anthracite veins that run beneath Scranton. Today, she rests at Saint Catherine's Cemetery in Moscow. Still, her memory is enshrined in the countless lives she touched—a perpetual flame of dedication and love in the hearts of those who walked the halls of the University of Scranton. Like the coal of her beloved Pennsylvania, her story is a rich seam of communal memory, fueling the spirit of care in the infirmary she founded, a legacy that, like her memory, will never dim.

3.22 Margaret Cicerini
Estate

Margaret Cicerini, now in her mid-80s, reflects a lifetime of quiet dedication to the Jesuit community at the University of Scranton. Though it has been years since she walked the corridors of the former Scranton estate professionally, her legacy of service remains a cherished chapter in the University's history.

Back when Margaret was part of the support staff, her role, although not headline-making, was the kind that kept the wheels turning. She was part of a team that ensured everything at the estate ran as it should. From setting up for events to maintaining the beauty and order of the surroundings, Margaret's work supported a building and its people.

The expectation for Margaret and her colleagues was one of excellence — to perform their duties quietly but effectively, ensuring that the Jesuits could carry on with their spiritual and educational missions without worry. The role demanded attention to detail, commitment, and a spirit of service — qualities that Margaret had in abundance.

Even though it's been years since Margaret held her position, those who remember her know it was more than just a good job. It was a calling that she answered with grace and diligence. Her

Unsung Pillars of the University of Scranton

work helped to uphold the Jesuit tradition of service and education, contributing to an environment where learning and spiritual guidance could flourish.

Today, Margaret's contributions are part of the institution's rich tapestry. Her story may not be widely known, but it is deeply appreciated by those who understand the value of her behind-the-scenes role. Her dedication during her working years left an imprint that resonates with the community she served so well.

3.23 Thomas Clark
Residence Halls

In the spirited embrace of the University of Scranton, a figure like Thomas Clark likely moved with purpose and pride, though the specifics of his tenure are not etched in any record. This essay attempts to honor the essence of what his days might have involved, drawing from the narrative fabric of the ordinary yet indispensable role he played.

Imagining his life in 1972, we picture Thomas beginning his rounds in dawn's calm, serene breaths. The residence halls stood as his charge—structures of learning and living where hundreds of students found their temporary abode. His task was monumental, not in the might of heavy machinery but in the consistent application of elbow grease and a can-do spirit.

His duties, while unrecorded, can be surmised as a mix of the routine and the unforeseen—the fixing of a jammed window, the unclogging of a well-used sink, the painting over scuffs and scrapes of exuberant college life. Each light bulb he replaced, each floor he swept, and each leak he fixed contributed to the unseen but deeply felt heartbeat of the campus.

Without concrete data, we can only construct a probable narrative of Thomas's professionalism and toil. He was likely the

Unsung Pillars of the University of Scranton

unsung hero who worked diligently to ensure that the residence halls remained more than just buildings; they were vibrant, clean, safe spaces conducive to the growth and development of the students they housed.

The story presented here, interwoven with the details imagined from a typical day in the life of a maintenance professional like Thomas, is an homage to the quiet dedication and integrity of those who work behind the scenes. It is a respectful supposition that captures the spirit of a job well done—a job essential to the smooth running of an institution as dynamic as a university.

While we may not have the exact records of Thomas Clark's service, the composite image we create is one of a steadfast steward of the halls of Scranton, a man whose work, though unlauded, was crucial to the enduring legacy of the University. It stands as a tribute to the importance of every role in an educational institution, recognizing that the strength of a university lies not just in its intellectual pursuits but also in the daily efforts of people like Thomas, who kept their hearts beating with unwavering commitment and care.

3.24 Marilyn Coar
President's Office

In a tucked-away office steeped in the hum of daily academia, Marilyn Coar was a fixture as enduring as the ivy-clad walls of the University of Scranton. Her story is woven into the institution's fabric—a tapestry of dedication and service. Her journey with the University began in the vibrant post-war years when the world was rebuilding and education was a beacon of hope.

Marilyn's role at the University was as multifaceted as the woman herself. She was not just the corporation's secretary; she was the unseen hand that kept the cogs of governance turning smoothly. As Assistanttive Assistant to the president for trustee affairs, she was the bridge between lofty ideals and grounded practice, ensuring that the board's vision for the University's future was not just a dream cast in the halls of power but a plan set in motion.

Her professionalism was a silent testament to her character, meticulous attention to detail, and unwavering commitment to the University's ethos. She upheld the sanctity of the boardroom with the same reverence she held for her faith, serving as a Eucharistic minister with solemn grace.

Unsung Pillars of the University of Scranton

Marilyn's early life was marked by achievement and a thirst for knowledge. Her academic prowess, evident from her days at Scranton Central High School, carried her to Rosemont College, where she graduated with distinction. Her leadership was apparent early on as she steered her classmates through their first year of college life, and later, as the president of the student body, she shaped student governance with a deft hand.

Her love for music echoed through the halls and corridors long after the notes had faded. She was not just an administrative powerhouse but a patron of the arts, nurturing the cultural heartbeat of the University.

In 1973, the University recognized her years of unwavering service with the 'Pro Deo et Universitate' award—a fitting accolade for a life thoroughly entwined with the institution's spirit. To Marilyn, the University was not just a workplace but a community, a family, and a part of her very identity.

Her final days were spent quietly at Dunmore Health Care Center with the dignity that had marked her life. Her legacy at the University endures a quiet force of nature that shaped the lives of countless individuals. She now rests with the blessings of her family and faith in the serene grounds of St. Catherine's Cemetery, Moscow, leaving behind a legacy that echoes in the hallowed halls of the University of Scranton.

3.25 Betty Connor
Cafeteria

Elizabeth A. Connor's story speaks volumes about dedication, a legacy of love, and a testament to her tireless work ethic, both in the heart of her home and the hubbub of the University of Scranton's cafeteria, where she served through the ARA food service firm until retirement.

Born into the dawning era of the 20th century, Elizabeth saw the world change in myriad ways, but her commitment to the constants in life - family, and service - never wavered. From 1907 to 1978, she was a cornerstone of her community in Taylor, Pennsylvania, where she lived and breathed the essence of giving.

Every day, after hours of managing the bustling university cafeteria, ensuring that students were nourished and ready to tackle their studies, Elizabeth would return to her abode. The aroma of home-cooked meals filled the rooms, a clear signal of her unwavering commitment to her large family - six sons and three daughters who awaited her culinary comfort.

Her evenings continued her day job, but the rewards were more intimate. As she peeled, diced, and simmered, she was also shaping her children's lives, instilling in them the values of hard work, persistence, and the importance of fulfilling one's role with pride and joy. The dinner table was often a conference room where lessons were taught, stories shared, and plans made.

Elizabeth's involvement with Saint Ann's Monastery church and the Saint Ann's Society wasn't just a commitment but a reflection of her deep-seated belief in community and faith. Her spirituality was a quiet strength that underscored her every action, a well from which she drew the patience and grace to manage her dual roles with aplomb.

Had fate allowed, she would have celebrated a half-century of marriage, a dance of partnership and mutual support with her husband that was cut just short of its grand milestone. Yet, in her fifty years of marriage, she had built a foundation for her family that would last generations, a structure of love and dependability.

Her life was not just about the meals prepared or the tables cleaned at work and home but about the lives she touched and the model of excellence she embodied. Elizabeth A. Connor was not merely a worker or a mother; she was a beacon of her time - her legacy a patchwork of the meals she crafted, the values she championed, and the love she served in generous helpings.

3.26 Gerald Connors
Long Center

Gerald Michael Connors, a stout-hearted man of Scranton, Pennsylvania, lived as solid and understated as the anthracite veins that run deep beneath the town's storied soil. With hands weathered by coal and a spirit undeterred by the rigors of labor, he wove his story into the fabric of Scranton, a tapestry of toil and resilience.

Born to the rhythm of the coal trains in the early 20th century, Connors's roots were as Scranton as the Electric City's streetcars. Education came in modest classrooms where life's lessons were as vital as reading and writing. He carried the lamp of knowledge from those schoolrooms to the dark tunnels of the mines, embodying the town's work ethic as unyielding as the coal itself.

The coal dust never settled on Connors's ambitions; it was a mere interlude in a life destined for diverse paths. From the depths of the earth to the driver's seat of the local bus company, he charted a course of occupational metamorphosis, steering clear of complacency. Yet, at the University of Scranton, he found his final calling, tending to the athletic facility with the same steadfast dedication he applied to every endeavor.

Unsung Pillars of the University of Scranton

A devout man, Connors's faith was as integral to his being as his love for Scranton. Saint Patrick's Roman Catholic Church knew his footsteps well, as did the brethren of the Holy Name Society, where he practiced his faith not just in prayer but in the fellowship of community service.

The patriarch of a family as closely knit as the coal community he sprung from, Connors was a husband and father first and foremost. His legacy, carried forward by two sons and a daughter, was one of unwavering support, ensuring that the fruits of his labor nourished his offspring's immediate needs and dreams.

In the end, as the pages of his story returned to dust, Connors's interment at Cathedral Cemetery was a silent testament to a life lived with purpose. His was a journey of many facets, each reflecting an aspect of Scranton itself—its grit, grace, and unspoken promise that every man's work echoes in eternity. Gerald Connors was Scranton, through and through.

3.27 Paul Conlon
Long Center

When the world was rapidly changing, Paul Jerome Conlon represented the steady pulse of the average workingman in Scranton, Pennsylvania, during the 1970s. A son of Carbondale, born into the roar of 1921, Paul was a man whose hands told the story of his life—a story etched in the calluses of hard work and the grease stains of dedication. When the Long Center at the University of Scranton needed someone to trust with its bones, they called upon Paul. His days, a rhythm of maintenance routines, echoed the man's reliability.

Paul's life was not without its trials. The echoes of World War II were a chapter he bore in silence, a testament to his strength and a past he shared with many of his time. He had known love, married in the rush of 1941, only to face the solitude of loss when his wife departed this world in 1949. The resilience of his spirit saw him through, for not only did he survive her but continued to thrive for his son and daughter, ensuring their survival was as inevitable as the solid ground of Dunmore, the suburb he called home.

His community was his extended kin, with ties to the Victory Post 13 American Legion, where stories of courage and sacrifice were common currency, and to Christ the King Church, where he sought solace and shared faith. In Scranton, the 1970s unfurled with a sense of recovery and progress, yet for the workingman, it was a period of continuity, of persisting in the face of a changing world.

Paul J. Conlon's life was a tribute to the era he embodied, when the American Dream was nursed in the hearts of those who toiled with their hands, upheld their communities, and, above all, persevered. His passing in 1972 at the Veterans Hospital in Wilkes-Barre closed the final chapter of a life lived in earnest, leaving behind a legacy woven into the very fabric of Scranton, a city that was, in many ways, a reflection of Paul himself— resilient, steadfast, and enduring.

3.28 Robert Defazio Jr.
Cafeteria

Robert Defazio Senior was a familiar stitch in Scranton's history, woven through the coal dust and family dinners. Between 1920 and 2002, he charted a path from the depths of the mines to the warm glow of a family-owned pizza restaurant, his hands shaping more than just the destiny of his kin. To the community, he was the mail carrier who knew every face, the businessman who served up slices of home. To his family, he was the bedrock, steadfast through fifty-six years of marriage, a father whose love was as generous as the portions he plated up.

His story is one of transformation — a life that moved to the rhythm of change yet never lost its tune. A graduate of Archbald High School and Lackawanna College, his education went beyond books; it was written in the soot and sweat of his youth, in the resilience of a man who carried letters and, later, the cargo weight for Roadway Express. His son, Robert Defazio Junior, found his footing in this narrative.

The year is 1972. The University of Scranton buzzes with the energy of young minds, but down in the cafeteria, where the scent of fresh coffee mingles with the steam of hot trays, Robert Jr. serves more than just meals. He serves memories, a piece of the legacy left by his father. His duties may be to ensure that no student goes hungry to keep the silverware shining and the counters clean, but his responsibilities run deeper. Each tray he balances is a testament to his father's balance of work and warmth; each smile he offers to a homesick freshman reflects Senior's enduring kindness.

While the specifics of Robert Jr.'s time in the cafeteria remain out of the spotlight, the essence of his service is illuminated by the life of Robert Sr. — a life of devotion, not just to his work but to his family, including two daughters whose own stories weave through Scranton's tapestry. The values Senior embodied — perseverance, hard work, and a commitment to community — are the unseen ingredients in every meal Junior served.

In the absence of records, the spirit of Robert Defazio Senior fills the gaps, painting a portrait of a man whose legacy is not just in the jobs he held but in the life lessons he imparted. For those who knew him or those who simply know of him, his tale echoes through the clatter of dishes and the hushed conversations of a university cafeteria, where his son, a silent guardian of the family narrative, continued the story.

Unsung Pillars of the University of Scranton

3.29 Frank Dipietro
3.30 Thomas Dipietro
Cafeteria

The DiPietro family laid their roots deep into the community's soil in the heart of Dunmore, Pennsylvania, nestled between the folds of bustling streets and the echoes of church bells. Frank and Thomas DiPietro were the heartbeats of their family's catering business, not just kin but comrades in arms. With hands seasoned by spices and hearts marinated in familial love, they stood as testaments to the quintessential Italian family bond—a tapestry woven with threads of unwavering loyalty and the rich colors of tradition.

Their journey wasn't captured in ledgers or menus but in the warm smiles of satisfied customers and the clatter of dishes in the University of Scranton cafeteria, where their work ethic was as much a staple as the marinara sauce graced the spaghetti. Frank and Thomas, with sleeves, rolled up and aprons dusted with flour, were more than just employees; they were custodians of the community, guardians of gastronomy, fostering a sense of home for every student and staff member lined up for a taste of their heritage.

They moved with the grace of seasoned chefs and the warmth of uncles at a family gathering, turning the university cafeteria into an extension of their dining room. Their labor was a dance, a ballet of pots and pans, where every meal was a performance worthy of an ovation. The DiPietro brothers didn't just serve food; they served memories, dollops of comfort spooned onto every plate.

Their fellow employees were not just colleagues but an extended family, each person a unique ingredient in the DiPietro recipe for camaraderie. The laughter that bubbled up amidst the steam of cooking pots was as nourishing as the food itself. The bonds of a shared heritage and collective pride were forged in the clinking of glasses and the sharing of shifts.

Frank and Thomas represented the epitome of the immigrant narrative to the broader community, etching their American dream in the fertile ground of mutual respect and hard work. Their legacy was not written on parchment but in the lives they touched, the students they fed, and the community they built— one cannoli, one conversation, one shared hardship at a time.

For Frank and Thomas DiPietro, their work at the university cafeteria was more than a job; it was a continuation of a story that began across the ocean in the sun-kissed fields of Italy. It was a story of perseverance, family, and, above all, a reminder that the essence of community is not just found in the breaking of bread but in the hands that prepare it.

Unsung Pillars of the University of Scranton

Unsung Pillars of the University of Scranton

3.31 Frank Doherty
Saint Thomas Hall

In a corner of Scranton, under the ever-changing skies, Frank Robert Doherty laid his mark in the most unassuming ways. His hands, though worn, were never weary, for they worked in service of a place that shaped minds and futures. Frank was part of the Maintenance Department at the University of Scranton, a cog in a machine that hummed with academic life. He was behind the scenes, ensuring that the halls of learning stood firm and that every light bulb banished the dark from students' desks.

His story, woven into the fabric of the University, was honored in 1984 with the Order of Pro Deo et Universitate, a testament to two decades of dedication. Frank's roots ran deep in Scranton, born to the coal-dusted breeze of 1911; his life's journey ended in the same town eighty years later. His youth was interrupted by the tumult of World War II, where he served with the Army Air Force, braving skies far from the Pennsylvania haven he called home.

Before his years at the University, General Electric had known the precision of his work. Yet, it was not the machines or systems that defined Frank but his unwavering commitment to the community he cherished. A steadfast figure at Saint Mary of the

Assumption Church, he was more than a parishioner; he was a pillar that others could lean on in times of need.

His was a life of service, not just to God, but to his fellow man. As a member of the Knights of Columbus, the American Legion, and the Veterans of Foreign Wars, he embodied the spirit of camaraderie and patriotism. These were not titles or mere memberships but extensions of his character, the essence of his being.

Frank was a family man at home, married with a son, his legacy evident in the quiet strength and love he bestowed upon them. His life, one could say, was a masterclass in the art of being a solid citizen, a good family man, and a loyal employee. He walked the earth with a sense of purpose and left it with a trail of gentle footprints, indelible and profound.

Frank Doherty might not have been a man of grand gestures or public accolades, but his impact was immeasurable. He embodied the unsung hero who believed in the dignity of work and the importance of community. His life was a mosaic of simple acts and steadfast duties, each piece a testament to a well-lived life. In Scranton, in the heart of the University, the spirit of Frank Doherty lives on, whispering through the corridors, a reminder that every task, no matter how small, is a stitch in the tapestry of humanity.

Unsung Pillars of the University of Scranton

3.32 Robert Doherty
Student Center

Robert G. Doherty, a name not etched in the marquee lights of fame yet inscribed in the annals of the humble city of Scranton, carries a story that is uniquely his and emblematically American. A son of Scranton, born as the Roaring Twenties dawned, his life was a tapestry of service, art, and dedication, woven into the broader fabric of a generation that came of age during the tumultuous times of World War II.

In 1942, as the world was engulfed in the throes of a war that would redefine borders and spirits alike, Robert donned the uniform of the U.S. Army. He was part of the 112th Cavalry, a unit that faced the brunt of battle in the dense jungles and unforgiving terrains of the southwest Pacific. For two years, he was away from home, immersed in experiences that would carve out the contours of his character. His service, marked by courage and camaraderie, was a testament to the grit of the men who fought and the enduring bonds they formed.

Upon returning, these veterans brought resilience and a perspective that would enrich their communities. Robert was no different. When he returned to Scranton, he got the same sense of commitment and duty he displayed in the military to his work at ARA Service for the University of Scranton. For 16 years, he

Unsung Pillars of the University of Scranton

served the institution, becoming a part of its growth and a figure of reliability and honor to those who knew him. His time there, until his passing in 1989, was not just a job but a continuation of his service to the country, now transmuted to service to education.

The post-war era saw these veterans step into roles that would shape the future, carrying with them an unspoken understanding of work not just as a means to an end but as a calling. Robert's work ethic and the depth of his experience were imprinted on the University of Scranton, echoing the contribution of his entire generation to the workforce. They were the quiet custodians of progress, the silent architects of the present.

Robert's story did not start with the war or end with his return. Scranton was where he learned the value of community, attended Central High School, and discovered his love for art, a passion pursued at the Arts Student League in New York City. These experiences, bookends to his time in service, were the sources of solace and expression for a man of few words but deep feelings.

In 1948, Robert married, weaving another strand into his life's tapestry, one of love, companionship, and shared dreams. Together, they navigated the post-war world, building a life in the city that had shaped him.

He now rests at the Cathedral Cemetery in Scranton, his gravestone a quiet sentinel to a life lived with honor, a life that speaks of the everyday heroism of a generation that asked for little yet gave so much. Robert G. Doherty's story is etched in the city's memory, a gentle reminder of the ordinary people who lead extraordinary lives, their legacies not in the grand gestures but in the steadfastness of their daily toil.

Unsung Pillars of the University of Scranton

3.33 Mary Donly
Estate

Mary Charlotte Donly's life weaves a tapestry of service and family—a tale of a woman whose hands shaped both the hearth and the hallowed halls of the University of Scranton. Born in the brisk dawn of 1912, she grew amidst the coal-strewn landscapes of Dunmore, Pennsylvania, her spirit as enduring as the anthracite beneath.

A graduate of Dunmore High School, Mary's education was an ember that ignited a lifelong pursuit of knowledge and community. It was within the ivy-clad embrace of the University of Scranton that she found her calling. For years, Mary was the sinew and the soul of the estate staff, tending to the needs of an institution in the throes of growth.

The year 1977 marked a milestone when the University lauded her dedication—a recognition not just of years served but of moments: the soft shuffle of her footsteps in the early hours, the swipe of her dust cloth that captured both dust and worries, and the gentle authority she wielded like a wand of care.

Though steeped in service, Mary's life found its cornerstone in her family. She was the matriarch of a bustling household, with two sons and two daughters, each a distinct chapter in her book of life. Her hands, calloused from work, were also instruments of love—cradling, guiding, and nurturing her children amidst the laughter and tears of a home ever alive with the symphony of family.

The tapestry of Mary's world took on shades of solitude in 1985 when widowhood draped its cloak over her. Yet, her resilience never wavered. She found the rhythm to dance through life in the echoes of her children's footsteps. Her son, steadfast in the service of the local police force, mirrored her dedication to community—a trait as inheritable as the twinkle in Mary's eyes.

A devout congregant of Saint Mary of Mount Carmel Church, Mary also embroidered her faith into her days. The Women's Guild benefited from her grace and wisdom, her actions a silent sermon of her beliefs.

Mary Charlotte Donly, a woman of modest beginnings, built a legacy that stretched beyond the confines of Dunmore. Her journey from the corridors of education to the pews of devotion, from the warmth of her family home to the solitary strength of her later years, was a pilgrimage of purpose. Her life—a narrative of dedication—continued until 1991, leaving behind the echoes of a mission well-embodied and a life well-lived.

3.34 Kathleen Dunleavy
Registrar's Office

In the heart of Scranton, where the bustle of academic life thrives amidst the red-brick buildings of a venerable institution, there once toiled a woman whose life was as interwoven with the city's history as the cobblestone lanes are with its present. Her name was Kathleen Noone Dunleavy, a name not known to the world at large but one that echoed with significance within the halls of the University of Scranton.

Born into the cradle of the coal city, Kathleen was a product of Scranton Technical High School, class of '34. Those were the days of the Great Depression, a time when the very fabric of America was threadbare, and yet, through sheer determination and the unspoken resilience characteristic of her generation, she found her way into the workforce, first within the Scranton tax collector's office, and later, as fate would have it, at the University itself.

In 1945, love blossomed amidst the backdrop of a world at war, and Kathleen married a man who had served his country in the Army Air Force, returning from the southwest Pacific after long months away from home. Their life together was a tapestry of shared moments and a growing family with three sons and a daughter to call their own.

She became a widow in '97, a prelude to her departure a year later. Still, the story of Kathleen's life is not one of sorrow but of service - a legacy etched not in stone but in the countless schedules and transcripts she meticulously managed in the Registrar's office. There, amid the clatter of typewriters and the soft shuffle of paper, Kathleen's contribution to the University took shape.

The Registrar's office was a nerve center where the pulse of academic life could be felt with every course registration, every grade recorded, and every degree conferred. Kathleen was part of that intricate ballet of administrative tasks, a guardian of records, a facilitator of futures. Her days were spent in the methodical and precise care of students' academic records, ensuring that the i's were dotted, the t's were crossed, and each form and file found its rightful place in the grand ledger of education.

Her work was more than a job; it was a calling, and in recognition of her unwavering dedication, the University bestowed upon her the Order of Pro Deo et Universitate, an honor reflecting her deep commitment to God and the University.

Yet, perhaps Kathleen's most cherished role was that of a mother and grandmother, her devotion to her family a beacon that guided her through the years. Her boundless and nurturing love was her most significant legacy, which would outshine even the most commendable professional achievements.

Unsung Pillars of the University of Scranton

Now, Kathleen Noone Dunleavy rests in Cathedral Cemetery, her spirit enshrined beneath the Scranton sky. But amidst the records and registries, her memory endures within the university archives, a silent testimony to a life of quiet dedication to her family, her city, and the hallowed halls of Scranton's seat of learning.

3.35 Doris Edsell
Data Processing

In the mosaic of American life, each tile shines with its hue and story. In the heart of Scranton, a tile glinted with the determined spirit of Doris Marie Lowry Edsell, a beacon of modernity in a world just waking up to the hum of computers.

Doris, born in 1922, was a product of Scranton through and through. Her life, a tapestry woven with threads of innovation, began humbly within the walls of Scranton Technical High School. From there, she charted a path less traveled by her peers, especially women of her time. Doris's journey through the echelons of Capitol Records, IBM, and Federal Pacific wasn't just a job—it was a calling.

The 1970s found Doris at the helm of the data processing function at the University of Scranton. In those days, data processing was an art as much as a science, a field where punch cards were the brushes and massive, room-sized computers were the canvas. A keystroke was a deliberate act. A punch card held the weight of intent. Doris navigated this world with finesse, understanding that each card sorted and each tape whirring in the mainframes was building towards the digital age.

Unsung Pillars of the University of Scranton

Her role was multifaceted: she translated the binary world of computing and the University's academic needs. She oversaw the delicate ballet of data—input, processing, and output. In this developing field, where women were more often the exception than the rule, Doris stood as a vanguard. She embodied precision and foresight, ensuring that the University's academic and administrative needs were met and anticipated.

Doris's life wasn't confined to the flickering lights of computer rooms. In 1943, she joined her life with Robert Wesley Edsell, and together they turned their melodies into a harmonious symphony. Their family grew, as did their roots in the community of Scranton, with Doris's involvement in the Church of St. Joseph, Minooka, where she was not just a member but a pillar in its women's societies.

The world shifted, and computers shrank from giants to gadgets resting on desks, but Doris's legacy was indelible. In 1980, the University of Scranton gave her the Pro Deo et Universitate award, a testament to her unwavering dedication. Her life, woven into the fabric of Scranton, came to a close in 1996, but the echo of her keystrokes resounded much longer.

Now, she rests in Saint Joseph's Roman Catholic Cemetery in Minooka, her gravestone a bookmark in the annals of a city that grew alongside her. In Scranton, where the memory of coal dust still lingers, Doris's story reminds us that those who dare to punch the first card often write the future.

Unsung Pillars of the University of Scranton

3.36 Jane Emery
Placement Office

In the bustling hallways of the University of Scranton, 1972, Jane Emery sat at her desk in the Placement Office, a linchpin in an environment pulsing with the dreams and anxieties of students. Her role, often unseen yet indispensable, wove into the fabric of this mid-sized Catholic institution, where tradition met the burgeoning change of the 70s.

Jane's day began with the clatter of typewriters and the ringing of phones, a symphony of administrative tasks that she orchestrated with a finesse born of experience. Her desk was an island of calm in the frantic ocean of college life, piled with folders of potential job listings and resumes of hopeful students. She was the bridge between academia and the real world, a guide who helped shape the uncertain paths of young adults stepping into a rapidly evolving job market.

In an era where women were carving their places in professional spaces, Jane's role was more than clerical; it was a statement of resilience and capability. Her expertise in handling confidential information, her knack for organizing career fairs, and her meticulous eye for detail in resume critiques all spoke of necessary professionalism and a quietly powerful influence.

Unsung Pillars of the University of Scranton

The Placement Office was a nexus of hope and opportunity, and Jane, with her ever-present smile and an uncanny ability to remember every student's name and story, made it a welcoming haven. She understood the weight of her responsibility – each file she handled, each appointment she scheduled, was a step in someone's life journey.

Lunchtimes were brief respites, often spent at her desk with a sandwich in one hand and a phone in the other, scheduling interviews or counseling a nervous student. Her dedication was a silent testament to the era's ethos – work was not just a job; it was a mission, especially in an educational institution where every action rippled into the future of society.

The office's pace slowed as the day waned, but Jane's work continued. She meticulously filed away documents, ensuring that every piece of paper was in its rightful place, a guardian of dreams and opportunities. In the quiet of the evening, she would finally step out of the office, the corridors echoing with the footsteps of a day well spent.

In the grand narrative of the University of Scranton, Jane Emery might have been a footnote, yet to those who passed through the doors of the Placement Office, she was a defining presence. Her professionalism, warmth, and unwavering commitment to her role painted a vivid picture of the importance of an administrative assistant at such a crucial juncture of life and education. She was a beacon of guidance in an institution standing at the crossroads of tradition and change, embodying the spirit of an era that valued diligence, respect, and the profound impact of helping shape a student's future.

3.37 Martha Evans
Cafeteria

Martha Evans' story unfolds in the bustling backdrop of a university cafeteria, nestled in the heart of the University of Scranton, where the echoes of youthful aspirations meet the unyielding rhythm of daily sustenance. It was the early 1970s, and the world outside was a tapestry of change, yet time held a certain constancy within the cafeteria walls.

With hands that worked tirelessly, Martha was one of the many women who formed the backbone of this institution. Her day began when the sun barely hinted at the day ahead, and the campus lay in slumber. She was part of a symphony of clattering trays, the hiss of steam, and the murmur of students whose names she knew but whose stories often passed her by in the rush of mealtime.

For Martha, the cafeteria was more than a place of employment; it was a theatre of life where she played a pivotal yet understated role. She served hundreds of dorm students, each one a world unto themselves, with the efficiency and warmth that only someone who understands the gravity of their role can provide. Her job was demanding, an unceasing dance between counters and kitchen, balancing the tightrope of quality and quantity.

Unsung Pillars of the University of Scranton

The women who worked alongside Martha shared a silent bond woven through their understanding of their dual lives. Their work at the cafeteria was a chapter in their more significant story, one of providing for families, of nights spent worrying over a sick child, and mornings spent ironing uniforms for school. They were caregivers, breadwinners, and unsung heroes whose labor was as nurturing as necessary.

In a mid-level Catholic institution, where values were etched into the very architecture, the contribution of Martha and her colleagues was a quiet testament to the ethos of service and community. Their presence was as comforting as the meals they served, a reminder that the human touch sustained the spirit even in the relentless pursuit of knowledge.

Martha's world was one of invisible threads connecting the tapestry of the university community. She was a guardian of tradition, ensuring that even as the world outside churned with progress, the sanctity of communal dining remained untouched. Yet, for all her importance, she remained largely unnoticed, a figure in the periphery of the vibrant campus life.

The life of Martha Evans is a mosaic of moments many would not recount, but it is in these unspoken narratives that the true essence of a community reveals itself. Her story is a gentle reminder that history is not only made by those who stand in the spotlight but also by those who ensure the spotlight continues to shine.

3.38 Mary Farrell
PBX (Switchboard)

In the heart of the University of Scranton, nestled amidst the hustle and bustle of academic life in the early 1970s, a heartbeat kept the flow of communication steady and sure. In a room that buzzed with the sound of connections being made sat Mary Farrell, the University's PBX (Private Branch Exchange) switchboard operator, her fingers dancing across the board with a rhythm that was as essential to the campus as the professors in the classrooms.

Before emails, text messages, and direct calls were within reach, Mary was the linchpin in the vast web of campus communications. Her role is to understand a world where a missed connection could mean a missed opportunity. She was the voice that greeted every inquiry, the hand that connected every call, the ear that heard the needs of the many faces she may never have seen. Her switchboard was her instrument, and she played it with the finesse of a seasoned maestro.

The switchboard was a complex apparatus, a board of jacks and cables that required a deft touch and an attentive mind. Each plug connected a call, each light a person waiting, each switches a path to someone's day being made more accessible. In an era before digital displays and automated voices, Mary knew each connection by heart, her mind mapping out the campus extensions better than any guide could.

Her duties were not handed down in manuals or taught in training sessions. Mary was self-taught, a testament to the ingenuity and resourcefulness required when one's role was learned through the doing, not the telling. She was a figure of trust, her discretion as much a part of her role as her ability to connect calls. Confidentiality was not just professional; it was personal.

Mary Farrell, though her name may not be etched in the University's official annals, was a vital cog in the daily operations of the University of Scranton. She held a position of unsung importance, ensuring that the lifeblood of information flowed freely and effectively. In a time when the personal touch was the standard, she embodied the very essence of reliability, attention to detail, and an unwavering commitment to service.

In recounting the story of Mary, we remember not just a person but a time, a place, and a role that was crucial in the days before modern technology transformed the landscape of communication. Through her, we see the switchboard operator as a job and a cornerstone of an institution's daily life. Her legacy is the understanding that behind every functioning system, there are individuals whose contributions are the foundation of all success. Mary Farrell, the switchboard operator of the University of Scranton, was indeed one such individual.

Unsung Pillars of the University of Scranton

3.39 James Farrell
Print Shop

In the heart of a mid-sized Catholic university, nestled amidst the rolling hills of Scranton, was a bustling print shop that served as the lifeblood of the academic community. This was the era before the digital age when ink and paper weren't just mediums but messengers of knowledge.

James Farrell, a figure whose story is woven from the threads of gossip and the remnants of a bygone era, was at the helm of this print shop in the 1970s. The shop was a hub of ceaseless activity, where the clatter and hum of machines filled the air, blending with the scent of fresh ink. James, whose presence was as integral to the shop as the presses themselves, was known for his meticulous attention to detail and a steadfast commitment to his craft.

In a print shop of that time, particularly within a university setting, the roles and responsibilities were as varied as the courses offered by the institution. Staff was tasked with creating everything from scholarly journals to exam booklets, from event flyers to campus newsletters. These items were the tangible manifestations of the University's academic pulse, essential for communication and education.

Unsung Pillars of the University of Scranton

Employees like James were expected to possess a unique blend of precision, patience, and a tireless work ethic. They had to be agile problem-solvers with a keen eye for typographical errors and layout issues, ensuring every page reflected the University's commitment to excellence. Beyond technical skills, a sense of camaraderie and an ability to work under deadlines were critical.

Before the advent of digital communication, print shops were the vital organs of information dissemination. They ensured that knowledge was not just a privilege of the few with direct access to the lecturers and the library but a right of the many, distributed through the printed word.

The legacy of these print shops and people like James Farrell extends beyond the documents they produced. They were guardians of a tradition that honored the written word and its power to educate, inform, and inspire. While the digital age has transformed the way knowledge is shared, the ethos of the print shop lives on in the dedication of those who continue to value the craft and the message.

In these remembered stories of James and his print shop, we find a reflection of an institution's spirit, a testament to the enduring importance of the printed word, and an homage to those who diligently worked behind the scenes, shaping the intellectual legacy of a generation.

3.40 Louise Fetterolf
Faculty Offices

In the shadow of the anthracite-dusted hills of Scranton, there thrived a soul, Louise Pedrick Fetterolf, as steadfast as the coal beneath. Her narrative was not inscribed in the ephemeral ink of prominence but in the enduring ledger of daily toil and unwavering devotion to her community.

Born as the world grappled with the Great Depression's tail, Louise's tale began in 1925 in the heart of Scranton, Pennsylvania—a town as rugged and warm as the hearths it fueled. The daughter of Scranton's soil was a 1943 alumna of the Central High School, her young aspirations humming with the promise of the era.

The echo of World War II's end found Louise in the bookkeeping department of the International Salt Company. Here, amidst ledgers and figures, she found her calling in the meticulous art of numbers. But the heart seeks variety, and Louise's journey took her to the hallowed halls of the United Church of Christ, where her grace and efficiency as a secretary were as much a part of the church as the pews and the pulpit.

Her most storied chapter was at the University of Scranton, where she served as the science faculty's secretary in the corridors where science and inquiry danced. Before the digital age transformed parchment into pixels, Louise was the indispensable nexus of communication and administration. Her typewriter clacked the symphony of progress, her files a testament to an era's intellectual pursuits. She was both compass and anchor to the faculty, navigating them through the administrative seas and grounding them in the academy's ethos.

Louise's faith was as much a part of her as her gentle smile. At Hickory Street Presbyterian Church, she wasn't merely a member but a pillar, serving as an elder with a spirit as immovable as the church steeple. Her commitment was not of the superficial Sunday variety but a deep, abiding force that shaped her and, in turn, shaped others.

At home, her life's melody was harmonized by the laughter and challenges of raising two sons. Through their eyes, her legacy endures not in monuments or grand accolades but in the quiet dignity of a life well-lived.

Louise's journey concluded at 91 in the same town that gave her breath, leaving behind the echo of her diligence and the warmth of her presence. Her husband, a fellow traveler in the walk of life, had preceded her in rest by fifteen years, leaving Louise to carry their shared memories alone.

Her tale, woven into the tapestry of Scranton's history, remains a humble yet significant thread in the larger fabric of American life. It's a vignette of a woman whose existence was a testament to the quiet heroes who nurture, support, and uphold the many facets of our world, often unnoticed but forever necessary.

Unsung Pillars of the University of Scranton

Unsung Pillars of the University of Scranton

3.41 Lawson Force
Saint Thomas Hall

In the early 1970s, the halls of Saint Thomas at the University of Scranton echoed with the footsteps of many, but few as steady and unassuming as those of Lawson Force. A name not etched into the annals of the University's history. Yet, a presence that contributed to the institution's lifeblood, Lawson embodied the quiet pillars supporting grand edifices.

Lawson, a man likely nearing his mid-forties, wore the years on his face with dignified resilience. His background was as unpretentious as his demeanor; perhaps he was the son of a coal miner emblematic of Scranton's dynamic spirit, or maybe he descended from a line of hardy farmers who worked Pennsylvania's unforgiving soil. Whichever his lineage, it instilled in him a work ethic as steadfast as the anthracite veins running beneath the town.

His expectations for employment were modest – not for him the dreams of grandeur or avarice. Lawson sought a steady job, a means to provide, and the quiet satisfaction of well-done work. At Saint Thomas Hall, he found it. Whether he was tending to the maintenance of the hallowed halls, ensuring the smooth running of the day's events, or offering a silent nod of encouragement to a passing student, Lawson's contributions were as integral as the bricks and mortar of the University itself.

He may not have been shaping young minds in the classroom or leading administrative charges in the boardroom, but Lawson Force was shaping the environment in which such pursuits thrived. His hands, though calloused, were the hands that turned the key to open the doors of education each morning. His back, though stooped, bore the weight of a catholic institution's silent creed: to serve, to maintain, to support, without need for acknowledgment.

In a time when the world outside was reeling with change – social upheavals, political dramas, and cultural shifts – Lawson represented a continuity. He was the steady gaze in a storm, the quiet force that, day in and day out, ensured the University was more than a mere structure; it was a living, breathing community.

Lawson Force's story is a composite sketch of countless unsung heroes. Men who clocked in as the sun rose and clocked out as it set, men who might not feature in the University's official portraits but without whom the portraits would hang on none but dusty, forgotten walls. In his ordinariness, Lawson was extraordinary, a testament to the legions of working men and women who, through their silent toil, are the bedrock upon which institutions rest.

3.42 Dolores Forkin
Registrar's Office

In the heart of Pennsylvania, where the anthracite coal whispers tales of the past, Dolores P. Forkin etched her life into the fabric of Scranton's history. Born in 1916, a time of world turmoil, she grew into a pillar of strength and reliability, her roots running as deep as the mines. A proud Scranton Technical High School graduate, she charted a course that would see her touch countless lives with a ledger in one hand and a spirit of service in the other.

Her journey through the tapestry of work began at the Consolidated Molded Products Corporation. There, amidst the hum of machinery and the meticulousness of numbers, she found her calling in the accounting department before the tides of love and commitment turned her to new shores.

1946 marked a milestone, the beginning of a union that would bloom into a large family, her dedication unwavering, her love an unspoken anthem to those she held dear. Yet, Dolores' story was not one to remain within the four walls of home. The University of Scranton's Registrar's Office became her realm, a place where futures were shaped, where her attention to detail and nurturing guidance left an indelible mark.

Unsung Pillars of the University of Scranton

But the threads of Dolores' life wove beyond the University's venerable halls. At VNA Hospice, she extended her touch, a comforting presence for souls in the twilight, her compassion a balm for both the departing and those left to mourn.

Faith was her compass, guiding her through the labyrinth of life's trials and triumphs. Holy Cross Church bore witness to her devout spirit, echoed with her voice in the choir, and saw her hands raised in prayer with the Altar and Rosary Society.

In 2003, the curtain fell on Dolores' earthly performance. Saint Catherine's Cemetery in Moscow, PA, embraced her with the same warmth she had extended to many throughout her life. A stone now stands, a testament to a life richly lived, quietly commanding respect not just for the roles she played but for the lives she touched, the institution she served, and the family she cherished. Like the anthracite of her beloved Scranton, her legacy endures—solid, invaluable, and irreplaceable.

3.43 Rosemary Fox
Treasurer's Office

Rosemary Fox worked in the Treasurer's Office of the University of Scranton, tucked away behind the grandeur of stately buildings and the rigorous academia of the 1970s. A beacon of steady competence in a sea of male scholars and Jesuit administrators, Rosemary's presence was as much a statement as it was a service.

To understand the perspectives of women like her, working at an all-male institution is to understand a silent revolution. They navigated corridors of power without the privilege of holding any. They sought respect and recognition, not just as employees but as equals, in a place that was slow to adapt to women's changing societal roles.

What they wanted from their positions was complex. It wasn't just a paycheck, but a chance to prove their worth, to contribute to something greater than the sum of its parts. They sought to be part of a community, expand their horizons, and challenge the status quo while performing their roles meticulously.

The management style that resonated with them was one of inclusion and acknowledgment. They thrived under leaders who saw their potential, provided opportunities for growth and learning, and valued their input as much as any other. A leadership that fostered a culture of mutual respect and fairness was the wind beneath their wings.

Their usual duties and responsibilities were as varied as they were vital. They balanced the books, managed finances, and interacted with the pulse of the University – its students and faculty. Each form filled, each account reconciled, and each student's query patiently answered was a testament to their unwavering commitment to the institution's financial health.

Like her contemporaries, Rosemary was not just a cog in the machine but a pioneer, quietly shaping the future of the workplace with grace, resilience, and an unspoken promise of hope for the women who would follow.

3.44 Jessie Furtini
Residence Halls

In a modest corner of the University of Scranton, Jessie Furtini swept through the halls with a grace that belied her day's toil. Born beneath the Tuscan sun in 1920, Jessie brought the warmth of Italy to the chill of Pennsylvania, where she became a steadfast figure in the housekeeping department, tending to the needs of a campus that was, for the longest time, an enclave for young men guided by the strict hands of the Jesuits.

Jessie's years whispered tales of the polished floors and the clean slate of desks before the day's lessons. Though the University was a male-only bastion, the women who scrubbed its pillars and paneled floors carried the place on their backs, often invisible yet indispensable. Their role, often unspoken yet keenly felt, was the heartbeat of an institution that thrived on order and discipline.

The housekeepers, Jessie included, were a quiet army in their own right, donned in aprons instead of armor, wielding mops as their scepters. They shared a camaraderie, a fellowship born of shared labor. To the Jesuits, they were the unseen gears in a clockwork of academia, but among themselves, they were the keepers of stories, the whisperers of dreams that echoed off the walls they washed.

Unsung Pillars of the University of Scranton

Jessie, a widow since '82 and a mother, held her head high, her dreams for her child as bright as the surfaces she polished. Her aspirations were simple yet profound – to see her child succeed, to live a life unburdened by the toil that marked her days. She found worth in her work, the order she brought to chaos and the cleanliness that was her silent signature on the fabric of the University.

Yet, there was dissonance in the air they breathed, a sense of being undervalued that clung to their uniforms. The labor was back-breaking, the hours long, the acknowledgment scarce. They were unseen. Their presence was felt only in their absence. The unappealing lay in the shadows of recognition, in the quiet disregard of their tireless efforts.

When Jessie passed in 1996, she left behind the scent of lemon on wood, the sheen on marble that reflected decades of young men who would become the movers and shakers of the world. She is buried in Cathedral Cemetery, her tombstone a testament to a life of service, a life that was a whisper in the grand narrative of the University yet a roar in the hearts of those who knew the touch of her hands.

The dreams and aspirations of Jessie and her fellow housekeepers remain a mosaic of the unspoken desire for respect and acknowledgment, for a legacy that acknowledges that every brick and book in the grand edifice of education was cradled, at least once, by hands that cared, by hands like Jessie's.

Unsung Pillars of the University of Scranton

3.45 Edward Gallagher
Residence Halls

In a bustling corner of the University of Scranton, Edward Gallagher's presence was as steady as the brick walls of the residence halls he tended to. The early 1970s was a time of change and growth for the university and the world outside its campus. Edward, a man with a quiet demeanor and a steady hand, was responsible for maintaining the dormitories, ensuring that the student's home away from home was safe, clean, and functional.

His days were filled with the humdrum of maintenance tasks: fixing leaky faucets, ensuring the heating worked during harsh winters, and attending to the myriad of small but crucial jobs that kept the halls running. But Edward's role was more than just a caretaker of buildings; he was a silent guardian of young lives. He moved through the halls with purpose, often unnoticed but always observant.

The students, caught up in the whirlwind of their academic and social lives, rarely acknowledged Edward's efforts. Some did, with a nod or a quick "thank you," but to many, he was just a part of the scenery. Yet, he watched over them with a paternal eye. He worried when they seemed stressed during exam periods and felt a sense of pride when he saw them laughing and enjoying their youth.

Edward's feelings towards the university were complex. He was proud to be part of an institution that shaped the minds of the future, but a part of him longed for recognition. He didn't seek accolades or fanfare; a simple acknowledgment of his hard work and dedication would have sufficed. He knew the importance of his role, even if others didn't always see it.

His neighbors and family saw his job as a stable, respectable position. It provided for his family, a significant achievement in a community where steady work was not taken for granted. His family was proud of him, understanding the dedication and effort he put into his job.

Edward's aspirations were simple yet profound. He wanted to be treated with respect and dignity, not just as a background figure in the university's day-to-day life. He hoped for a future where people in roles like his were seen and appreciated, not just for their labor but for their contribution to the larger community.

If Edward could have recommended it for the future, it would be for a culture of mutual respect and acknowledgment. He would advise that everyone deserves recognition and appreciation, no matter their job. In his eyes, every role was vital to the university's success, and everyone, from the professors to the maintenance staff, played an integral part in shaping the students' lives.

Edward Gallagher left an indelible mark on the University of Scranton in his quiet, unassuming way. His story is a testament to the unseen heroes in our midst, whose daily toil lays the foundation for our brighter tomorrows.

Unsung Pillars of the University of Scranton

Unsung Pillars of the University of Scranton

3.46 Mary Gallagher
Admissions Office

Mary Gallagher's office at the University of Scranton, with its neatly stacked papers and the soft hum of a desk fan, was a quiet testament to the unseen cogs that keep an institution running. The early 1970s were a period of change and challenge, yet Mary's steady presence in the admissions office remained a constant.

She didn't make speeches or head committees; her work was quieter but less vital. Each application that crossed her desk was met with a thoughtful gaze and a meticulousness that spoke volumes of her commitment to the university's future. It wasn't just about grades or accolades; Mary looked for something more intangible in potential students – a spark, a hint of the resilience and character needed to thrive in academia and life.

Colleagues remembered Mary as someone who spoke little but observed much. Her insights, often shared in a low, earnest tone during staff meetings, would sometimes steer the course of admissions decisions in profound ways. She had an uncanny ability to see potential where others saw uncertainty.

Though not etched in the grand annals of university history, Mary's legacy lives on in the generations of students she touched.

Unsung Pillars of the University of Scranton

Some became leaders, thinkers, and changemakers, carrying a part of that silent wisdom imparted through her discerning choices.

To the outside world, Mary Gallagher was just another employee in the admissions office. But to those who knew the university's inner workings, she was a linchpin, an unsung hero who quietly shaped the University of Scranton's future with every application reviewed.

Unsung Pillars of the University of Scranton

3.47 Louis Gallo
Long Center

In the early 1970s, within the bustling corridors of the University of Scranton's athletic center, Louis Gallo, a figure of quiet strength and unwavering commitment, became a staple. His exact role remained a mystery to many, yet his presence was as essential as the walls of the facility. Louis, a son of Italian immigrants, carried with him not just the dreams of his family but the collective aspirations of a community deeply rooted in the values of hard work and familial bonds.

For Louis, the athletic center was more than a workplace; it was a microcosm of the life he knew. Each day, he witnessed young students, much like himself years ago, striving for excellence, driven by their ambitions and the expectations of their families. Louis saw in these students a reflection of his journey, a narrative deeply entwined with the Italian immigrant experience in Scranton.

In Scranton's Italian community, commitment was not just a virtue but a necessity. Families clung to each other, their bonds forged in the fires of shared struggles and hopes. Louis's approach to his work was a mirror of this ethos. He treated every task and every interaction with the meticulous care and deep respect it deserved. His dedication was palpable whether he managed equipment, offered advice to a struggling student, or ensured the facilities were in top shape.

His work ethic, a blend of the traditional Italian values instilled by his parents and the lessons learned in the immigrant neighborhoods of Scranton, became his guiding principle. Louis believed in the power of hard work, not just as a means to an end but as a testament to one's character. To him, each sweep of the broom, every neatly arranged set of weights, was an homage to his heritage, a tribute to his parents sacrifices.

But beyond the ethic of hard work, family was the cornerstone of Louis's world. In the close-knit Italian community, family extended beyond blood relations. It encompassed friends, neighbors, and, in Louis's case, the students and staff he interacted with daily. His approach to work was deeply intertwined with this sense of extended family. He looked out for the students as if they were his own, offering guidance, a listening ear, and sometimes a gentle nudge in the right direction.

Like many Italian immigrants in Scranton, Louis's story was not one of individual triumphs but collective resilience. His commitment at work reflected a more significant commitment to his community and family. In the echoes of the athletic center, amidst the sounds of bouncing balls and distant cheers, Louis Gallo stood as a testament to the enduring values of hard work, family, and community. This legacy transcended the bounds of his unknown role.

Unsung Pillars of the University of Scranton

3.48 Rose Marie Giambrone
Estate

In the heart of Scranton, where the forge of the industry once roared, Rose Marie Frattali Giambrone found her rhythm, a cadence marked by service and the hum of a steadfast spirit. Born in 1920, when the world was caught between wars and the Great Depression loomed on the horizon, Rose Marie grew with the century, her roots entwining with the coal-streaked soil of her birthplace.

Her early education at Saint Francis Cabrini and Scranton Technical High School provided the framework for a life dedicated to the community. The war years saw her stepping forward as a volunteer with the American Red Cross, her hands and heart aiding those in turmoil. She contributed to the war effort at the General Electric Corporation. Her work there is a testament to the era's call for women's strength.

Post-war Scranton unfurled into an era of growth, and Rose Marie grew with it, her life weaving through the city's fabric. At the University of Scranton, within the hallowed halls of the Jesuit Estate residence, she became more than an employee; she was a guardian of tradition, an embodiment of the institution's values.

Volunteering with the Parents Club at the West Side Boys Club, she nurtured the youth, and her involvement with the Scouting

Unsung Pillars of the University of Scranton

program ensured the passage of her values to the next generation. Politics, too, felt her touch, her four-decade tenure as a Democratic committeewoman reflective of her belief in civic duty and the power of the collective voice.

Yet, the family held the heart of Rose Marie's world. Cherishing her two children, she wove a tapestry of love and memory that would remain their heritage long after her passing in 2007, following a long about with cancer. Her legacy is one of resilience and devotion, of a life spent in service to others, her final rest in Cathedral cemetery a mere pause in the narrative of a prosperous life.

Rose Marie Frattali Giambrone's story is not just one of personal triumphs and public service; it reflects Scranton, a city of hardworking, passionate people who give of themselves, build and rebuild, cherish their past, and foster their future. In her story, we find the story of every person who has ever loved a place, a community, or a family and made it their life's work to leave it better than they found it.

Unsung Pillars of the University of Scranton

3.49 Virginia Gilboy
Best Sellers

In the tapestry of Scranton's history, there's a weave not of thread but of words and paper, meticulously crafted by Virginia Mary Gilboy. A woman whose name became synonymous with 'Best Sellers,' the esteemed book review birthed from the intellectual fervor of the Catholic Library Association. In the quiet corner of her world, Virginia was the circulatory system that gave life to its pages, ensuring that, twice a month, over three thousand eager minds received their share of literary guidance.

She held not just lists of subscribers but the pulse of an era that valued the written word as a beacon of culture and knowledge. It was 1941, and the world was at war, yet within the University of Scranton, Virginia, the team cultivated an international conversation on literature.

Her name was perhaps uttered in the same breath as the latest literary treasures for many years. Her dedication saw 'Best Sellers' burgeon into a tapestry of reviews penned by over three hundred stewards of literature from thirty-six states.

Even as the tides changed, with the passing of Rev. Edward J. Gannon, S.J., and the university's retracting support in the wake of financial pragmatism, Virginia's commitment remained unwavering until the end of the publication's tenure.

Unsung Pillars of the University of Scranton

Scranton was not just her home but the stage of her life's work. A Saint Cecilia High School graduate, she was woven into the city's fabric, as enduring as the texts she helped disseminate. Clarks Summit knew her as a resident, a neighbor, and a friend for thirty-eight years, steadfast as the books she championed.

Marriage, for her, was not a chapter but the very theme of her life, one of love and partnership that endured for forty-nine years until her husband's departure, a testament mirrored in the longevity of her career.

Her legacy? It isn't just in the written words or the silent rows of library shelves that her work helped populate. It's in the memory of her son, in the hushed reverence of Saint Joseph's Cemetery in Minooka, and in the hearts of all those who knew the quiet power of a woman who orchestrated the symphony of Scranton's literary heartbeat.

Unsung Pillars of the University of Scranton

3.50 Lena Giordano
Residence Halls

In the heart of Scranton, amidst the changing times of the early 1970s, a period marked by vibrant social shifts and the slow but steady march towards gender equality in educational institutions, Lena Giordano stood as a beacon of nurturing guidance. She was a figure of stability and care in the University of Scranton, which, like many others, was navigating the significant transition from being an all-male bastion to welcoming women into its fold. This was when the term 'dorm mother' still carried weight, and Lena, embodying this role with grace and resilience, became much more than the title suggested.

Lena, a Scranton native, was a product of the very schools that had shaped the minds of many of the city's young. She was well-versed in the values and expectations of her community, grounding her in the unique position to serve as a bridge between the traditional values of the past and the emerging realities of a coeducational future. As a widow, having faced the heartache of loss when her husband passed in 1967, she brought to the role a depth of empathy that only personal grief can cultivate. This experience, while deeply personal, became a wellspring of compassion that she extended to the students under her care.

Unsung Pillars of the University of Scranton

The role of a dorm mother at that time was complex and multifaceted. Lena was not merely an overseer of rules and a regulator of conduct; she was an advisor, a confidante, a mentor, and, to some, a surrogate parent. Her presence in the dormitory was a comforting constant in a world where young men and women were grappling with the challenges of academia and the social upheavals of the day. Lena's charge extended beyond ensuring the smooth running of dorm life. She took it upon herself to be an educator of life skills, a listener to those needing an ear, and sometimes a firm hand to those needing guidance.

Her wisdom was dispensed in the lounges and hallways, over shared meals, and during those late-night chats that only seem to happen within the confining walls of a dormitory. Lena's life, with its joys and sorrows, was an open book from which students learned lessons of resilience, the value of education, and the importance of community.

The transition to coeducation was not without its trials and trepidations. Lena stood at the helm of this change, ensuring that the integration was as seamless as possible. She was instrumental in fostering an environment where both men and women could thrive academically and socially, respecting each other's space and dignity. Lena was a pioneer in a world that was just beginning to understand the richness that coeducation could bring.

Her tenure at the university saw the weaving of a new social tapestry, where the threads of tradition and progress intertwined under her watchful eye. When Lena passed away in 1999, she left a legacy in the lives of the countless students she had nurtured. She had been a child of Scranton, a widow of sorrow, a mother not just to her child but to many, and above all, a silent architect of a more inclusive and compassionate academic world.

Unsung Pillars of the University of Scranton

Her memory, etched in the annals of the university's history, continues to inspire the ethos of care and community that she championed.

Unsung Pillars of the University of Scranton

Unsung Pillars of the University of Scranton

3.51 Stanley Gorski
Loyola Hall

In the early '70s, the University of Scranton was a tapestry of stories woven from the myriad threads of its community. Stanley Gorski was one such thread, a vibrant yarn spun from the coal dust of the mines to the hallowed halls of Loyola. His was a familiar tale in those days; the miner's lamp traded for the janitor's keys, a transition from the earth's dark veins to the academia's enlightened corridors.

Once blackened with coal, Stanley's hands found new work in the university's service. He was one of many men who carried the weight of blue-collar legacies into their twilight years, not in search of glory but in the quiet pursuit of steadiness as their working sunset. To them, the university was not just an employer but a chance at reinvention, a transition from the muscle-tiring toil to the dignity of maintaining an institution of learning.

He wasn't one to wax poetic about his role; for Stanley and his peers, appreciation was a luxury, secondary to family provision and honest work satisfaction. Yet within the university's embrace, they found a camaraderie, a silent acknowledgment of their worth beyond the measure of their labor.

Unsung Pillars of the University of Scranton

As years etched lines on his face, marking each smile and each season of hardship, the university grounds became a witness to the life he carried forward from the depths of the mines. The gratitude of the faculty and students may not have always been overt. Still, it was woven into the very fabric of the every day – the clean floors, the tended gardens, the smooth operation of a place dedicated to higher thought and greater good.

Stanley's story continued a quiet narrative until 1988, when his chapter concluded in Ohio, far from the university's stone-clad buildings. A life member of the United Mine Workers, his faith as steadfast as his work ethic, he was a man of the Nativity of Our Lord Church, where belief and community were his refuges.

His marriage, a testament to enduring partnership, nearly saw its 53rd year, a union that mirrored his long-standing ties to the labor he performed with such resolute dignity. In death, he returned to the earth, not to the dark tunnels of his youth but to the hallowed ground of Saint Mary's Church in Greenwood, where his story, etched on a headstone, lies amidst others who shared his journey – from the dust of the earth to the custodianship of an institution, from the depths of labor to the heights of service.

3.52 Madelyn Gorsline
Residence Halls

Madelyn C. Gorsline, born in the springtime bloom of 1910, carried the essence of her era — a blend of resilience and grace. Stitched together like a quilt of simpler times and communal ties, her life found its rhythm within the walls of the University of Scranton's residence halls. Here, she moved, not merely as a housekeeper but as a guardian of the students' home away from home.

Her days were unfurled with the sunrise, bringing a fresh canvas of untidy dorm rooms each morning. With a practiced hand, she swept away the remnants of youthful disarray, her mop dancing over linoleum floors, her duster flirting with the dust motes in the slanting light. Beds were made taut, each corner a testament to her meticulous care. Windows gleamed, mirrors shone, and the air, once stale with the remnants of late-night studies and laughter, turned crisp, as if she'd captured a breeze from the nearby Pocono Mountains and folded it into the room.

Madelyn's presence was a quiet constant, often unnoticed until absence whispered the weight of her role. She was the unseen hand that steadied the chaos of college life, the silent ally in the quest for knowledge. To some, she was a background figure in their collegiate memories, yet to others, her smile was a beacon of maternal warmth, her words a scaffold of support.

Widowed, Madelyn wove her life with the threads of community and faith. The local bridge club became her arena of camaraderie and competition, where laughter was both a shield and a salve. Each game was a tapestry of strategy and fellowship, where she wasn't just Madelyn, the widow or the housekeeper, but Madelyn, the intelligent card player, the beloved friend.

Her devotion found another home within the Church of Nativity. She served as an Altar and Rosary Society member with a humble heart, finding solace in the rituals and the rose-scented prayers that rose like incense to the heavens. Her faith was as much a part of her as her steadfast nature, offering a well of strength from which she drew her patience and compassion.

When her chapter closed in the winter of 1983, Madelyn left behind more than just the echoes of her footsteps in the hallways of the university. She left imprints on hearts, subtle but memorable. She rests now in the Cathedral Cemetery, beneath the sky she once mirrored in her polished surfaces, surrounded by the community she cherished, her spirit as much a part of the place as the statues that watch over her in silent vigil.

In the tapestry of the University of Scranton's history, Madelyn C. Gorsline is a subtle yet integral thread, her life a testament to the quiet pillars of our communities, whose contributions, often unnoticed, are the foundation upon which the grandest structures stand.

Unsung Pillars of the University of Scranton

3.53 Robert Grambo
Student Center

In the heart of Scranton, in the bustling student center of the University of Scranton, Robert F. Grambo was a figure as integral as the beams that held the building upright. A maintenance worker by trade but a caretaker by nature, he saw the rise and fall of countless semesters, each with its own set of young, bright-eyed scholars. His hands, calloused but gentle, fixed leaky faucets and creaking doors ensured that academic life flow went unimpeded.

Beyond the walls of academia, Robert shared his life with his beloved wife, and together, they were the heartbeat of a small variety store in Scranton. It was more than a business; it was a gathering spot where locals found what they needed: warm smiles and listening ears off the shelves.

1983 saw Robert and his wife donning the red suit and snowy beard, embodying the spirit of Santa Claus for a holiday event, their laughter and joy a beacon for the Pennsylvania Association for the Blind. They became the season's unsung heroes, giving gifts, hope, and a sense of community.

1973 marked a milestone that filled Robert's chest with indescribable pride. His son, Ralph W. Grambo, not only achieved the lofty title of Doctor of Philosophy from the prestigious University of Pennsylvania but also returned to the academic embrace as an associate professor for business administration. It was a rare accomplishment that made a father's heart swell with pride.

This pride was twofold, as Ralph had also honored their family by serving as an officer in the U.S. Army. This path started with the ROTC program at the very university where Robert dedicated his working days.

Robert's journey ended on Independence Day of 1985 in the quiet confines of the Scranton bus terminal. A day that symbolizes freedom and celebration bore the weight of mourning for those who knew and loved him.

He was laid to rest amidst the green serenity of Fairview Memorial Park in Elmhurst, a stone among many, but to those who knew him, a monumental figure. His story remains etched in the hearts of his family, friends, and the community he served – a legacy of service, love, and an undying pride for a son who soared academically and served his country with honor.

Unsung Pillars of the University of Scranton

3.54 Joyce Greco
Athletics Office

Joyce Greco is not headlined in the sports pages yet etched deeply in the annals of the University of Scranton's athletic history. In the bustling athletics office of the 1970s, where the hum of typewriters was as rhythmic as the bounce of a basketball, Joyce was the unsung hero whose work behind the scenes was pivotal to the university's sporting success.

The University of Scranton's athletic programs, particularly in the early '70s, were a burgeoning force in NCAA Division III sports. Under the dim fluorescents and amidst the clatter of office chatter, Joyce's hands were on the pulse of this athletic heart. She was a linchpin, one might say, in a machine that thrived on enthusiasm and elbow grease as much as talent and coaching.

Imagine a time when sports administration was as much about ledger books as game books. Joyce's role in the athletics office was more than administrative; she was a weaver of community, threading relationships between students, faculty, and the wider Scranton community through the power of sports. Her dedication was as critical to the department as any coach's strategy or player's performance.

Unsung Pillars of the University of Scranton

The Scranton Royals men's basketball team, which clinched the Division III NCAA Championship in 1975-76, was a testament to the robust program Joyce helped sustain. The triumph on the court reflected the victories of the countless hours of meticulous planning, organizing, and promoting that Joyce and her colleagues dedicated to the department.

Today, the University of Scranton's athletic department remains a vibrant part of the university's ecosystem, boasting 23 sports teams. The continuity from those formative years in the '70s is unmistakable, a thread that weaves through the fabric of time. Joyce's legacy lies not just in the department she helped shape. Still, in the ethos of commitment and community, she instilled – an ethos that continues to underpin the success of the university's athletics program.

In the collective memory of the University of Scranton, Joyce Greco is remembered as the cornerstone of an era that laid the foundations for decades of athletic prowess – a time when the victories were as much hers as they were the university's.

Unsung Pillars of the University of Scranton

3.55 Ray Gregos
Cafeteria

In the early 1970s, within the bustling heart of a mid-sized Catholic college, the University of Scranton, a world was often unnoticed yet fundamental to the daily rhythm of campus life. This world was the college cafeteria, a hive of activity, aromas, and sounds, where a team of dedicated workers orchestrated the daily feat of feeding nearly a thousand dorm and commuter students.

Among these culinary conductors was Ray Gregos, a figure whose presence in the cafeteria was as constant as the morning coffee. Like many of his colleagues, Ray was part of a larger narrative of labor and community that colored the era. In a time when the roles in such environments were often sharply defined by tradition, men like Ray typically found themselves in roles that required strength and endurance - hauling supplies, managing the heavy cooking equipment, or overseeing the efficient operation of the meal service lines.

The team that Ray was a part of was not vast in numbers but immense in spirit. Each member played a crucial role, from those who meticulously prepared meals to those who ensured that every surface gleamed after the day's hustle. In a period marked by social and cultural shifts, the cafeteria staff sometimes

Unsung Pillars of the University of Scranton

felt the strain of their labor-intensive roles. Yet, there was a prevailing sense of camaraderie and purpose. They were not just employees; they were caretakers, fueling the minds and bodies of a generation poised on the cusp of change.

Ray worked with quiet dedication, speaking more through actions than words. His legacy was not one etched in grand gestures or accolades, but in the everyday reliability and commitment he brought to his work. For the students, many were preoccupied with exams, social lives, and the looming uncertainty of adulthood. Ray and his colleagues were steady. They offered sustenance and a semblance of home, a comforting routine in the whirlwind of college life.

As years passed and the faces in the cafeteria changed, the memory of Ray Gregos remained with those who knew him. His legacy, subtle yet enduring, was in the way he exemplified the dignity of everyday work, the quiet solidarity shared among his team, and the unspoken understanding that their labor was a vital thread in the fabric of the university's community. In the echoes of clattering dishes and the steam rising from hot plates, there was a story, a narrative of ordinary people like Ray, who, in their modest way, helped shape the experience of a generation in transition.

Unsung Pillars of the University of Scranton

3.56 Ethel Grimes
Cafeteria

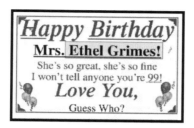

In the mosaic of Scranton's heart, a tile glimmers with a warmth reminiscent of home-cooked meals and the touch of a maternal hand. Ethel Grimes is a name spoken with fondness, a smile that graced the University of Scranton cafeteria, etched in the memories of those she served in the early 1970s. The scent of Thanksgiving turkey and the clatter of cutlery on plates echo the sentiment: Ethel was beloved.

The university was her stage, the cafeteria her domain, where students and faculty were her guests, her family. Each tray she slid across the counter carried more than sustenance; it held her affection, care, and love. She knew them all by name, their favorites, their quirks, and even those with a homesick glint in their eyes.

In 1970, the local paper captured the essence of Ethel's dedication. A pre-Thanksgiving meal at the university, a tradition she held dear, was not just a meal; it was a communal gathering, a momentary return to the warmth of a family table for many. Ethel and her fellow workers toiled joyfully to weave that magic.

Time ticked on, pages of the calendar turned, and in 1983, Ethel reached a milestone, her 70th year. The university women, who shared the laughter and occasional tears behind the scenes, orchestrated a celebration of life for Ethel and two of her contemporaries. It was a testament, not just too long, to longevity and in the daily dance of dishing out meals and exchanging pleasantries.

And then, a moment that transcended the ordinary. In 2012, when the crisp pages of the local newspaper bore an ad, it wasn't a mere announcement. It was a proclamation, a celebration of Ethel's 99th spring. The words were a tapestry of affection, a public declaration that she was more than a cafeteria worker; she was a thread in the fabric of the community, a weaver of bonds.

These vignettes, these snapshots of Ethel's journey, underscore the fundamental truth about the nature of work and connection. The bonds between employees and their employers, the sense of belonging, and the shared purpose are the underpinnings of a superb organization. Ethel Grimes embodied this ethos and lived it every day with every ladle of soup and every slice of pie served.

In a world that often overlooks the quiet contributors, Ethel's legacy is a reminder that the heart, the humanity, truly makes a place shine. Her belovedness was her gift to Scranton, a gift that, like the finest of meals, will linger long after the last plate has been cleared.

Unsung Pillars of the University of Scranton

3.57 Edward Hawley
Carpenter

In the heartbeat of Scranton, there was a man whose hands could speak to wood, a teller of tales through grains and grooves. He was the university's silent architect, shaping the spaces where young minds blossomed. In the 1970s, our carpenter's day would start when the morning was still a whisper, his toolbox a treasure chest of possibilities.

The campus was his canvas; he was not just a fixer of broken benches or a mender of desks worn by time and thought. He was a guardian of history, ensuring that each lecture hall and dormitory whispered the legacy of generations. His training, likely, was not from grand institutions but from life itself, hewn from experience, from watching and doing, from transforming splinters into smooth surfaces.

Appreciation in those days was more than words; it was the nod of a professor, the smile of a passing student, the silent thank you of a door that no longer creaked. He held a quiet pride in his work, a dedication seen in the corners of the rooms, in the joints and jamb of every frame he crafted.

His life was not just in the woodwork, but in the home he built, not from timber but from love and laughter with his family.

Unsung Pillars of the University of Scranton

Though he left us in the early '80s, his work lives on in the corridors of learning, in the sheltering arms of the Cathedral Cemetery, and in the hearts of those who knew him.

His legacy is that of every artisan who shapes the world in unassuming ways, whose signature is the integrity of their craft and the warmth of their heart. He was a carpenter, yes, but also a creator, a keeper of tradition, and a cherished memory in the annals of the University of Scranton.

3.58 Joseph Hoban
Library

Joseph Hoban worked in the hushed corridors of the University of Scranton library amidst the towering stacks of books and the ever-present scent of aged paper and wisdom. It was the early 1970s, and the world was teetering on the cusp of technological revolutions, yet within these walls, time moved to the gentle, methodical rhythms of a bygone era.

Joseph, a rarity in a domain predominantly staffed by women, found his niche within this scholarly haven. His days were filled with meticulous cataloging tasks, the academic pursuit of aiding research, and the stewardly duty of preserving knowledge. He was a guardian of information, an understated and paramount role, especially before the digital age illuminated the world with web services.

The importance of the library then cannot be overstated. It was a central hub, not just of academia, but of the community it served. The library was where the vibration of the outside world dimmed to a whisper, where one could delve into the depths of human thought and emerge hours later, enlightened and transformed.

Unsung Pillars of the University of Scranton

Joseph was instrumental in this transformation with his quiet demeanor and steady hands. He was appreciated, not in grand gestures or loud acclaim, but in the silent gratitude of students engrossed in study, professors immersed in research, and the gentle nod of his female colleagues who shared the unspoken bond of those dedicated to the service of knowledge.

His responsibilities were numerous: checking out and reshelving books, ensuring the card catalog was up to date — a painstaking process in an era where every new addition or subtraction demanded a physical alteration. He managed periodicals, the lifeline for keeping up-to-date with the evolving discourse of various fields. He assisted patrons with using microfiche readers, those bulky ancestors, to today's sleek digital databases.

In the age before the internet, every question sought through the library required a journey — through indices, directories, and sometimes a conversation with a knowledgeable staff member like Joseph. The librarians were the shepherds guiding the flock through the informational labyrinths. With his tacit knowledge and steady presence, Joseph was an anchor for those adrift in the sea of scholarship.

For Joseph Hoban and his colleagues, the library was a living entity, and they, its pulse. They kept the information available and accessible, a feat that now seems Herculean in its complexity and simplicity. The library of the University of Scranton was a beacon of knowledge, and Joseph, a quiet yet integral part of its legacy, contributed to the intellectual growth of countless individuals who passed through its doors, most unaware of the meticulous labor that kept the heart of the library beating.

Unsung Pillars of the University of Scranton

3.59 Harold Homer
Long Center

In the heart of Scranton, where the anthracite coal once fueled the nation's industry, Harold L. Homer carved out a life of quiet significance. Born to the city's hum of the early 20th century, Harold's story is interwoven with the very streets of Scranton, where he would become as much a part of the local landscape as the city's storied coal mines.

His journey with the Hudson Coal Company began as a young man, fresh-faced and eager. For 47 years, his hands dealt with the currency of hard work in the paymaster's department, counting wages to the men who toiled beneath the earth. He witnessed the industry's ebbs and flows, the coal dust mingling with the ink on his fingers, a testament to his commitment to his work.

Upon the closure of the mines, Harold found sanctuary in service through the University of Scranton Athletic Center. Here, he became an unassuming community pillar, a steadfast presence at the ticket seller booth, greeting fans with a nod and a smile as they came to cheer on the basketball team. His face became synonymous with game day, a comforting constant in a world prone to change.

Unsung Pillars of the University of Scranton

Faith was Harold's compass, guiding him through life's trials and triumphs. A devout member of Saint Mary's Assumption Church, he was deeply involved in the Holy Name Society and Saint Mary's Parish Society, where he found camaraderie and purpose. His faith was not just a solitary comfort but a shared celebration as he stood shoulder to shoulder with fellow parishioners, his voice among the chorus of hymns that filled the sacred space.

Perhaps the most defining aspect of Harold's life was his son, a Roman Catholic priest ordained in 1959. Harold's pride in his son's vocation was a beacon that lit up his world. It was a source of boundless joy, a testament to his love for his faith and family. His son's commitment to the church mirrors Harold's devotion, reflecting the values he held most dear.

In every ticket sold and prayer whispered, Harold L. Homer's legacy was etched into the fabric of Scranton. His was a life that, while never clamoring for the spotlight, shone brightly with the steady glow of dedication, faith, and familial love.

Unsung Pillars of the University of Scranton

3.60 Ann Hopkins
Residence Halls

In the heart of the University of Scranton, as the '70s ushered in flared jeans and vinyl records, a particular pulse in the residence halls echoed more than just the students' chatter. Ann Hopkins, a steward of these halls, might not be a name you read in history books, but her story is etched in the countless lives that bustled through the corridors of this Catholic, mid-sized university.

Ann was part of a team, a community within a community, where the concept of togetherness wasn't just preached. It was practiced. In those times, maintaining a residence hall was akin to tending a large, diverse family. The team approach was crucial, with each role interlocking with the other like a well-oiled machine built on a bedrock of shared values and mutual respect. This was especially true in a Catholic institution where every action was a testament to collective harmony and service ethos.

The women attracted to this type of work, like Ann, were often the unsung heroines of their day. They were women of resilience and warmth, often drawn not by the lure of acclaim but by the desire for steady employment that carried a sense of purpose. They sought to contribute to a community that fostered growth and upheld the spirit of unity — ideals that resonated deeply within the halls they maintained.

These women found happiness in the daily triumphs, the smiles of students relieved to find a lost belonging or the sigh of relief when tensions were dissolved with just the right words. They were pillars, not just of the buildings but of the lives that filled them. Their satisfaction was not in the job itself but in their impact, the small but significant ripples they created in the pond of these young adults' lives.

Ann's story is not documented in journals or on plaques, but her legacy is the lived experience of those she touched. It's a reminder that every cog in the machine, no matter how small, is critical to the movement of the whole. It's a testament to the team approach of those bygone days, where everyone played their part in shaping a generation, where faith met education, and where the hands that maintained the structures were as crucial as the minds nurtured within them.

Unsung Pillars of the University of Scranton

3.61 Ann Hoskins
Public Relations and Development

Amidst the academic spires of the University of Scranton, Ann Hoskins charted a course that was as much about perseverance as it was about pioneering. When she began her journey in the mid-century, the corridors of academia echoed with the footsteps of men in authority. At the same time, women like Ann typed their memos and managed their schedules.

From the day she stepped into the university, fresh from securing her secretarial degree from Lackawanna Junior College in 1941, Ann embraced her role with a zeal that would become her hallmark. Her tenure at the university saw her assuming various roles, each a stepping stone that paved her path forward, each position held with the dignity and dedication that came to define her.

Ann became integral to the university's narrative as she moved through the ranks, her contributions vital though often unsung. She was the voice that greeted countless inquiries, the hands that wove the fabric of daily affairs, and the mind that anticipated the needs of a growing institution.

Unsung Pillars of the University of Scranton

Then came the 1970s, a time of social upheaval and transformation, when Ann's steady rise met a crowning moment. After three decades of unwavering service, she was promoted to Assistant to the Vice President of Student Personnel, a role seldom bestowed upon women then, especially in the staunchly male-dominated environment of a catholic Jesuit college.

This elevation to the executive ranks was no mere change of title for Ann; it was a landmark of progress, a breakthrough not just for her but for all women in the echelons of higher education. It spoke of her resilience and ability to navigate the subtleties of a world that was gradually, and sometimes grudgingly, opening its doors to women in leadership.

Ann's ascent to the executive ranks demanded more than just competence; it required an unflappable conviction in her worth and a deft balancing of assertiveness with the grace expected of a woman of her time. Her legacy is etched not only in the annals of the university but also in the strides made towards a more inclusive future, a future she helped to write with every memo, every meeting, and every decision she was part of.

Unsung Pillars of the University of Scranton

3.62 George Houck
Long Center

George Houck, a sturdy figure often seen pacing the varnished floors of the University of Scranton's Long Center, carried within him the unspoken narrative of many middle-aged men of the early 1970s who found their calling in the humming activity of athletic facilities. With his calloused hands and a smile that spoke of quiet contentment, George believed in the sanctity of sweat and the rhythm of bouncing balls as a sort of symphony of effort and teamwork.

Those like George, who tended to the needs of these bustling centers, often harbored a profound connection with their work. It was not merely a job but a pivotal point of their identity. They saw themselves as custodians of the physical space and the spirit of camaraderie and growth that these places nurtured.

For George and his peers, there was a sense of pride in the polish of the court and the precision with which equipment was maintained. They felt an intrinsic reward in the seamless execution of their duties, which allowed young athletes to strive and sweat without worry. They weren't simply employees of the university but integral members of a community that pulsated with youthful ambition and raw talent.

Unsung Pillars of the University of Scranton

The university community, often preoccupied with academic and athletic pursuits, may not have always openly acknowledged the vital role these men played. Yet, there was an unspoken respect and appreciation in the slap of high-fives, the victorious yells echoing off the walls, and the quiet thanks from a coach for a well-maintained space.

To the outside eye, it might have appeared as a routine job, but for George, it was a chapter in his life where satisfaction came from the smooth functioning of a world geared towards molding the next generation. The Long Center was more than an athletic facility; it was a place where lives were shaped, and through his work, George became an unseen but essential artisan of human potential.

3.63 Mary Hyland
Graduate School Office

In the heart of Scranton, where the anthracite coal veins weave like arteries beneath the earth, Mary Margaret Hyland became a tapestry of the University of Scranton's history. It was 1951 when Mary first graced the corridors of the public relations office, her steps as measured and purposeful as the keystrokes of her typewriter. With every memorandum and every appointment she scheduled, Mary wove herself into the institution's fabric, becoming as indispensable as the books in the library.

Her odyssey through the university's many departments—the registrar's office, the development office, and the graduate school office—was a growth journey for her and the university itself. It was a time when the country was redefining itself, and so was Mary, embodying the change she wanted to see around her. The laurels of her education at Saint Patrick's High School and Lackawanna Junior College were not just framed certificates hanging on the wall; they were testaments to her lifelong commitment to learning and service.

Her pre-university days at the US Textile Company and the Hinerfield Realty company were but prologues to the story she would author at the University of Scranton. In a move as rare as a perfect diamond, the administration, recognizing the luster of

Unsung Pillars of the University of Scranton

her dedication and skills, promoted her to a professional position as assistant registrar for the graduate school. This position had always demanded the flourish of a college degree.

In 1974, the university bestowed upon her the Pro Deo et Universitate award, a gold medal not merely resting against her attire but reflecting the golden respect and admiration she had earned. Mary's legacy is inscribed in the annals of the university's history and in the hearts of those who walked the halls with her and benefited from her unwavering support and commitment to excellence.

Mary Margaret Hyland, born in the year when the world was recovering from the Great War, passed away as the 21st century found its footing. Yet, her spirit and dedication remain an unmovable stone in the foundation of the University of Scranton. Mary lived all her life in Scranton, but her influence extended far beyond the confines of the city, touching the future through the students and the community she served so diligently. Her story is not one of mere employment but of a life lived in full measure to the service of others, a life that continues to inspire long after her passing.

Unsung Pillars of the University of Scranton

3.64 Theresa Jasienesky
Residence Halls

In the embrace of the Pennsylvania mountains, Scranton unfolds as a town of unsung heroes and quiet labor. One such hero is Theresa Jasienesky, whose tapestry of life weaves through the hallowed halls of the University of Scranton, where she served with unwavering devotion in the early 1970s.

Theresa's story is rich with the texture of everyday life, the kind that often goes unnoticed. Yet, within the simplicity of her daily routines lies a profound narrative of love and commitment.

July 25, 1967, marked not just a date on the calendar but the silver celebration of Theresa and Stanley's marriage—a jubilee splashed across the pages of The Scranton Times. The photograph, now yellowed with age, captures more than a moment; it is a testament to a love that served as the bedrock for their family. Their six children, a vibrant bouquet of lives, grew up under the nurturing shade of this love. It was this same love that powered Theresa's days, a driving force that propelled her through the corridors and dorm rooms she tended to with care.

Though often invisible in the grand tapestry of the university's history, her work was foundational. Theresa's hands, worn yet gentle, smoothed the beds and swept the floors, ensuring the

Unsung Pillars of the University of Scranton

students' home away from home was welcoming. Her cleanliness and the warmth of maternal love permeated the residence halls.

In 1974, the university recognized Theresa with the Pro Deo et Universitate Award, an honor reflecting her service and the spirit with which she rendered it. This accolade was rare when the spotlight shone on someone who lived so much of life in the background, supporting countless young minds' dreams and academic pursuits.

Theresa's story is a mosaic of the era, reflecting a community of workers whose love for their families fueled their service. Her legacy and that of her peers at the University of Scranton endure in the fond memories of alums and the quiet dignity of the halls they once maintained.

The narrative of Theresa Jasienesky is one of silent strength and luminous love—a narrative that finds its deserved voice. It reminds us that the wealthiest stories lie within the overlooked corners of history, waiting to be told.

3.65 John Joyce
Saint Thomas Hall

In a city woven with the sinews of steel and the warmth of community, there was a man whose life embodied dedication and service. Let's talk about a fellow whose hands, calloused and capable, turned the wheels of progress in an institution that stood as a testament to knowledge and advancement.

This man, let's call him Mr. J., was a son of Scranton, born to the rhythms of a city that pulsed with the ebb and flow of coal and steam. In the crisp shadow of the Electric City's glow, he took his first breath in 1932 and would come to spend the majority of his days there.

He was a high school lad when he first stepped onto the university grounds, not merely as a student but as a worker, juggling the books with the honest toil of cutting grass and clearing snow, serving meals, and connecting calls at the switchboard. His was a life that began in service and remained so.

By '51, he was a graduate, not just of Central High but of the university itself, his alma mater in more ways than one. For 47 years, he would be a cornerstone of the institution, a quiet hero in the hum of the boilers and the buzz of the wires.

His journey was a familial affair, with his mother, aunts, and cousins all weaving their threads into the university's tapestry. Even his brother imparted wisdom in the history department. They were a family bound not just by blood but also by their shared dedication to this place of learning.

Mr. J. was more than just a worker; he was a scholar in his own right, earning a degree in business while maintaining the heartbeat of the university's physical form. And as he grew, so too did his responsibilities, from the man who mended what was broken to the one who oversaw the very sinews of the building's life—its electrical veins and breaths of air conditioning.

His life was not just cables and currents; there was love, too. He was a husband and father; his legacy is not just in the bricks and mortar of the buildings he maintained but in the lives he touched.

By '54, he was a name, a title—foreman, supervisor, the man to whom others looked when they needed assurance that the lights would turn on and the warmth would flow through the halls. In recognition of his steadfast dedication, the university honored him, etching his name into the very fabric of the campus with a building that bore his name.

Unsung Pillars of the University of Scranton

In '99, Mr. J. bid farewell to the city that had been his life's canvas. He rests now in St. Catherine's cemetery, but the hum of his work, the echo of his dedication, resounds through the corridors where he once walked, a perpetual reminder of what it means to serve, dedicate, and love a place and its people.

Let's remember him not just as a supervisor of systems but as a caretaker of a community's heart.

Unsung Pillars of the University of Scranton

3.66 Rosalind Joyce
Saint Thomas Hall

In Moosic, Pennsylvania, there's a quiet town where history whispers through the rustling leaves and the gentle streams, a town that is home to Rosalind P. Joyce. At 87, Rosalind is a living testament to the enduring spirit of commitment and the transformative power of a dedicated individual.

In the halls of the University of Scranton, where the echo of footsteps tells stories of times gone by, Rosalind began a journey that would span four illustrious decades. 2005 was a beacon in her life, recognizing 40 years of steadfast service. It was a celebration not merely of time but of the unwavering dedication that Rosalind poured into her work. Her induction into the Order of Pro Deo et Universitate was more than an accolade; it symbolized her life's passion, a narrative rich with dedication and purpose.

Rosalind witnessed firsthand the university's evolution from an all-male institution to a coeducational one, and she played a pivotal role in this transformation. She was not just a participant in this change; she was a catalyst. Her presence signaled a new era, where the once-exclusive halls of academia opened to the chorus of diverse voices.

Unsung Pillars of the University of Scranton

Through her tenure, Rosalind was a guiding light for the new generation of women who entered the university's gates — students and employees who looked to her as a paragon of possibility. In her, they saw a reflection of what they could achieve and the grace and tenacity required to do so.

Rosalind P. Joyce's life narrative extends beyond the boundaries of the University of Scranton, reaching into the heart of every individual striving to make a lasting impact. Her story celebrates resilience, the quiet power of persistence, and the revolutionary force of an unwavering presence. Rosalind's life is a reminder that one person's dedication can indeed move mountains and pave the way for future generations.

Unsung Pillars of the University of Scranton

3.67 Frank Kane
Residence Halls

In the residence halls of the University of Scranton in the early 1970s was a man named Frank Kane. The concrete details of his life—birth dates, milestones, the personal minutiae that biographers so often rely on—are lost to time, uncharted in the vast ocean of undocumented histories. Yet, this absence of record does not diminish the essence of his contribution to the university community; it underscores the universality of his presence, a figure representative of a generation whose personal accolades often went unspoken yet whose collective impact resonates through the decades.

The men of Frank's time, the "greatest generation," were sculpted by the difficulties of their era. Their characters were shaped by the harrowing experiences of war and their subsequent return to civilian life, where their actions spoke louder than any medal or commendation. At Scranton, these men found roles that perhaps lacked the grandeur of their wartime duties but were no less critical to the fabric of society. They occupied positions that required the blue-collar virtues of hard work, reliability, and steadfastness.

Though the annals of history may not recall the individual achievements of Frank Kane, his role at the university was a testament to the unsung heroism of his peers. These were the caretakers, the diligent workers whose every task, however mundane it might seem, was a brick in the foundation of an institution dedicated to nurturing young minds. Frank and his colleagues were the unseen gears in a great machine, their labor ensuring an educational community's smooth and continuous operation.

Frank's interactions with students were likely unrecorded, his guidance imperceptible at the moment, yet his influence was as accurate as the halls he walked. His generation's collective wisdom, their unspoken commitment to the future, was imparted not through lectures or textbooks but through the living example of their daily toil. They embodied a creed that valued integrity, service, and a commitment to something greater than oneself.

This narrative, while devoid of the typical markers of biography, is a homage to what Frank Kane and countless others brought to the University of Scranton: a commitment born of a harrowing past to ensure a promising future for the next generation. It is a story not of one but many, a mosaic of lives with quiet dignity. Frank Kane's name may not be etched in stone, but the ethos he represented leaves an indelible mark on the spirit of the community he served.

3.68 Peter Kapp
Long Center

In the heart of Scranton, where the University stands as a testament to both education and history, worked Peter W. Kapp. His story, woven into the fabric of the University, is a tapestry of service, loss, and resilience, emblematic of a generation whose youth was marked by global conflict.

Peter, a World War II veteran, served with distinction in the U.S. Navy Seabees. He brought the spirit of dedication and camaraderie to the University, a place that became a gathering point for many veterans of his era. They shared more than just memories of war; they shared a commitment to shaping a brighter future through education.

The university community knew Peter as an employee and a pillar of strength. His life took a heart-wrenching turn in 1969 when tragedy struck his family. His son, John Francis Kapp, followed in his father's footsteps of military service, only to fall in the Vietnam War. John's death in a fierce firefight during a resupply mission left an indelible mark on Peter. The loss of a child is a sorrow that never fades; it's a wound that time does not heal. Peter's son, who died serving his country, became a symbol of sacrifice and a reminder of the cost of freedom.

Unsung Pillars of the University of Scranton

Another loss marked Peter's personal life – the passing of his wife, who preceded him in death. Living as a widower, he carried both his private grief and the weight of history with a quiet dignity that spoke volumes to those around him.

Even in the face of personal tragedies, Peter's presence at the University was a source of inspiration. He represented a generation that had endured the unimaginable yet continued to contribute meaningfully to their communities. His colleagues, also veterans, found in him a kindred spirit, understanding the depth of his experiences and the strength it took to move forward.

Peter W. Kapp's final resting place is in Cathedral Cemetery, a place of eternal peace. His life, marked by service to his country and dedication to his community, remains a testament to the resilience and courage of those who have served. Like many veterans, his story is a poignant reminder of the sacrifices made by individuals and families for the greater good. In the halls of the University of Scranton, his legacy endures, inspiring future generations to carry forward the values of service, sacrifice, and perseverance.

Unsung Pillars of the University of Scranton

3.69 Joseph Kavelines
Cafeteria

In the heart of the University of Scranton's bustling campus, amid the ebb and flow of eager minds and youthful exuberance, worked a gentleman named Joseph Kavelines. With a warm smile and a knack for remembering faces, Joseph was a fixture in the cafeteria, where the aroma of coffee mingled with the din of student chatter.

The early 1970s, a time of vibrant change, had not spared the realm of food services. The winds of transformation blew through university halls, carrying with them the seeds of privatization. With their sleek operations and cost-cutting prowess, contractors were taking over, turning college kitchens into efficient, profit-driven ventures.

This shift was tectonic for the workers, especially men like Joseph, who had operated the stoves and counters for years. They watched as aprons were traded for uniforms and time-honored recipes gave way to standardized menus. Joseph, with his seasoned hands and a well-thumbed recipe book, could feel the ground shifting beneath his feet.

Yet, he adapted, as did his colleagues. They rolled with the punches, learning new systems and embracing the pace. If asked how they'd change the operation, they'd likely speak of a blend—

Unsung Pillars of the University of Scranton

keeping the efficiency but infusing it with the personal touch they prided themselves on, a touch that no corporation could replicate.

In the bustling ecosystem of the cafeteria, women were often at the helm. Joseph and his male peers witnessed this female-led domain with a sense of camaraderie. There was no talk of dominion, only respect for the matrons of the meal line, the queens of the cash register, who managed the daily dance of dining with grace and authority.

As plates clattered and silverware chimed, Joseph and his band of brothers in service worked in unison with their female counterparts, a symphony of sustenance that fed the body and the soul of a community in flux.

Unsung Pillars of the University of Scranton

3.70 Catherine Kelly
Residence Halls

In a town hemmed in by the anthracite richness of Pennsylvania's earth, Dunmore bred its inhabitants with a grit that matched the coal dusted under their nails. Catherine Mary Kelly lived among the close-knit homes peppered the streets like patchwork. Her story was not scribed in the annals of history books but was inscribed in the lives she touched within the walls of the University of Scranton residence halls.

To understand Catherine, one had to understand Dunmore of her time. It was a place where the air was often heavy with the hum of industry and the clang of progress. The people of Dunmore wore their work ethic like a second skin, toughened by the demands of their town's pulsing labor heart. It was not mere employment that drove them but a profound sense of community and solidarity.

Catherine was educated within the embrace of Dunmore's schools and carried this ethos into every bed she made and every floor she shone on at the university. Her hands, though worn, were never weary, moving with a rhythm that echoed the tireless spirit of her town. She served not out of obligation but with a pride that spoke of a deeper understanding of service. She was a custodian not only of the university's halls but also of the ethos that made Dunmore a forge of relentless workers.

Unsung Pillars of the University of Scranton

Her presence at the university was a silent sermon to the students, many of whom came from beyond Dunmore's borders. They observed, often unconsciously, the embodiment of a work ethic that was not taught in classrooms but demonstrated in the hallways and living spaces they occupied. Catherine's diligence was a living legacy, instilling in them a respect for labor's honest face.

Catherine's tenure at the university drew to a close as the years wove into decades, but the impression she left was indelible. When she passed away in the winter of 1983, the town of Dunmore didn't just lose a resident; it felt like the departure of one of its chapters.

Today, Catherine rests in Saint Catherine's cemetery in Moscow, PA, her name etched into stone, as her memory is into the hearts of those who knew her. The cemetery, a tranquil bookend to vibrant life, lies not far from the town that shaped her. Dunmore continues, its residents still carrying the torch of a work ethic that, much like Catherine's legacy, endures beyond the toll of the shift whistle.

Unsung Pillars of the University of Scranton

3.71 Dorothy Kennedy
Registrar's Office

In the heart of Scranton, where the anthracite coal once reigned, and the steeples of churches pierce the sky, there lived a woman who embodied the spirit of the community. Dorothy, a recorder at the University of Scranton, was a fixture in the registrar's office. Her days were spent in the hum of fluorescent lights amidst the rustling of transcripts and the steady click of typewriter keys. But it was not her work that defined her; it was the quiet strength she carried.

A widow since '66, Dorothy knew the sharp sting of loss, yet it never dimmed her smile or the warmth she extended to all. She graduated from the local high school, the kind whose memory was etched into the very sidewalks of the town.

Her faith was as much a part of her as her breath; Nativity of Our Lord was her sanctuary, and she served it with a devotion that was both earnest and humble. The Altar and Rosary Society benefited from her gentle leadership. Her hands are often busy with flowers or prayer beads.

Dorothy's legacy was not only in the records she meticulously kept but in the lives of her two daughters. In them, her qualities flourished - the resilience, the compassion, the unspoken understanding of what it means to be part of a community.

Unsung Pillars of the University of Scranton

Tragedy struck as sudden as a thunderclap in a clear sky on a summer evening. A cruel and unforgiving fire claimed the sanctuary of her Orchard Street home. Dorothy, who had spent the afternoon in her beloved church, succumbed not to the flames but to the shock of a heart that simply couldn't bear the loss. The fire consumed the physical, and the peace of a life so gently lived.

The town mourned, and the newspapers echoed the sentiment of a community heartbroken. To speak of Dorothy was to talk about kindness incarnate, a soul who had moved through life with a rare and understated grace.

She rests now in Cathedral Cemetery, among the rolling hills she had always called home. Her story is whispered in the hush of the pews, in the turning of pages in the registrar's office, and the quiet pride of her daughters. It's a tale not of how she left this world but of how she lived in it - with dignity, faith, and a love that lingers like the last light of day.

3.72 Bartley Klepadlo
Saint Thomas Hall

In the fabric of Moosic, a borough woven with the steadfast threads of coal and community, Bartley Klepadlo found his place among the looms of labor and loyalty. A lifelong resident, Bartley's story was much like the town—a tapestry of quiet determination and unassuming service. Moosic, nestled in the embrace of the Lackawanna County hills near the bustling city of Scranton, was where the work ethic was not merely an ideal but the very currency of existence.

The borough, with its streets lined with modest homes, the air often heavy with the memory of coal dust, was a testament to the generations who toiled beneath the earth and those who found their purpose above it. The residents, a proud and close-knit cadre, shared their joys and sorrows and the unspoken understanding that a day's work was worth more than the wage it earned—it was the measure of a person.

Bartley, a son of Moosic, carried this legacy with quiet pride. His days at the University of Scranton's Saint Thomas Hall were spent in diligent service, a role that might have seemed unremarkable to the unobservant eye but was essential to the tapestry of the institution. As the university's arms reached out to embrace a world of academia, the Bartleys of the place ensured its steady heartbeat.

Unsung Pillars of the University of Scranton

The nearby city Scranton was the larger stage where many from Moosic played out their professional lives. The journey from borough to town was a well-trodden path, a daily migration of ambition and necessity. The city offered what the borough could not—diverse jobs, broader opportunities, and a chance for sons and daughters of coal miners to pen new chapters.

Bartley's faith, as unwavering as his work ethic, found a home at Saint Mary's Church. The church's spire, a beacon amidst the borough's landscape, was as much a part of his life as his heartbeat. In death, as in life, he remained within Moosic's embrace, laid to rest in the soil of Saint Mary's Cemetery—a silent guardian of the place he never left.

He departed in 1986, leaving behind a brother and three sisters—silent witnesses to a man's life who sought no accolade for his contributions like so many before him. Those who had gone before him, a brother and two sisters, had already taken their place in the narrative of the borough's history, each leaving their indelible mark.

In Moosic, where the past is always present, Bartley Klepadlo's legacy is etched not in stone but in the living memory of the community he served—a narrative of a life rich in simplicity, a vignette of virtue that continues to whisper through the streets of the borough he called home.

3.73 William Kneller
Long Center

In the tapestry of northeastern Pennsylvania's past, the threads of countless lives weave a muted backdrop to the vibrant stories that history often recounts. In this quiet corner of the world, Scranton is a testament to the dynamic spirit that fueled its growth, a city whose anthracite coal once stoked the furnaces of a nation's progress. Yet, amidst the din of machinery and the clamor of a booming industry, the individual stories of its residents—like that of William Kneller, a 1972 employee of the Long Center at the University of Scranton—often remain untold, hidden in the folds of time.

These modest lives, unadorned with the fanfare of public record or familial lore, challenge us to listen closely and hear the echoes of their existence without concrete facts. The lack of verifiable information on individuals such as William isn't uncommon; it reflects a time and place where the daily grind didn't always merit a headline or a footnote in the annals of local newspapers.

In the early '70s, Scranton was a place of transformation, where the whispers of a bygone industrial era mingled with the burgeoning voices of education and culture. Like William, employees at the Long Center stood at the crossroads of this change. They likely shared the city's work ethic—a legacy of the

Unsung Pillars of the University of Scranton

mines and railroads—a resilience borne of necessity and a quiet determination.

Their outlook on life, while speculative, can be inferred from the community's character: pragmatic yet hopeful, hardworking, with a penchant for humble aspirations over grandiose dreams. They found joy in simple pleasures and weathered life's storms with a stoicism carved from the very coal upon which the city was built.

But the true spirit of Scranton's past lives on in the unrecorded tragedies, the personal triumphs, and the everyday moments of individuals like William Kneller. Their legacies, though not immortalized in print, are nonetheless integral to the city's story—a narrative of collective endurance, shared dreams, and the quiet dignity of lives lived in the service of community and family.

To seek the essence of Scranton's residents from half a century ago is to understand that, while many life experiences never graced the pages of newspapers, they were nonetheless rich and full. The tapestry of history may not always acknowledge each thread, but every life adds color and texture to the broader picture. Within this understanding, we grasp the significance of the uncelebrated, the power of the unrecorded, and the beauty of the ordinary.

3.74 Stephanie Kowalski
Residence Halls

In the heart-worn valleys of Lackawanna County, where the anthracite coal whispers tales of yesteryears, lived Stephanie Kowalski, whose hands, though they knew the toil of scrubbing and cleaning, were never too busy for a rosary's comfort at day's end. Born in 1916, a time when the world was churning with change, Stephanie's story is woven with the enduring threads of faith and labor.

Stephanie's youth was cradled within the walls of Sacred Heart School and Central High School, where the teachings of the Roman Catholic Church were as much a part of her education as reading and arithmetic. These steadfast and clear teachings left an indelible mark on her, shaping her into a woman who carried the virtues of diligence and charity through all avenues of life.

In 1941, love beckoned, and Stephanie answered, marrying her steadfast partner in life. Together, they weathered the storms and dances of the decades until he detached from the branch of life before her like a late autumn leaf.

Through the corridors of the University of Scranton, Stephanie's presence was a constant, a fixture as reliable as the morning sun.

Unsung Pillars of the University of Scranton

As a domestic worker assigned to the residence halls in the early 1970s, she was more than a janitor; she was the silent guardian of countless students' temporary homes. Her commitment to her work was a testament to the work ethic instilled by her faith. This faith reverberated through the region's culture, where church spires punctuated the skyline and community life.

The Roman Catholic Church, with its tapestry of societies and fellowships, found in Stephanie not just a member but a pillar. She participated fervently in the Christian Mothers and Blessed Sacrament society, found fellowship in the Catholic Golden Age Club, supported the Orchard Lake Auxiliary, and led as the past president of the Mother's Club of South Catholic Central High School.

The end of her labor came with retirement, but the fruits of her faith and work remained. She lived to see her children grow, to hold her values and lessons as heirlooms. A son and two daughters carried her legacy of resilience and devotion.

When Stephanie passed in 1987, it was not just a family that mourned but a community. Sacred Hearts of Jesus and Mary Church, her spiritual abode, opened its arms to receive her one last time before she was laid to rest in the Sacred Heart church parish cemetery in Minooka, PA.

Her story, etched into the memory of those who knew her and into the fabric of the region she called home, is a testament to the quiet strength and unwavering spirit of those who serve in humility and live in faith. Her life, a narrative not of grandeur but of genuine, heartfelt commitment, continues to echo through the halls she once tended to and the community she loved.

Unsung Pillars of the University of Scranton

3.75 Marie Kozik
Rehabilitation Office

Within the university's bustling corridors, a program thrived, dedicated to the art and science of healing not just the body but the mind and prospects of those dealt a harsher hand by life. At its administrative core was Marie Kozik, a figure pivotal yet modest, whose name may not resonate in public memory but whose influence pulses through the veins of the program she oversaw.

Marie's role was pivotal; she was the administrator who steered the ship through administrative challenges, weaving together the complex tapestry of schedules, curricula, and human resources. Her position was crucial, yet her leadership was not about being at the forefront but about ensuring that those who were—educators and students—had the foundation and support to excel in the field of rehabilitation counseling.

In the early 1970s, this field was a beacon of progress, a response to the growing recognition that recovery, in its truest sense, encompassed more than physical mending. It was about restoration—of dignity, of capability, of life's manifold opportunities. The Rehabilitation Office at the University of Scranton was a microcosm of this more significant movement, and Marie was its unsung guardian.

Unsung Pillars of the University of Scranton

As an administrator, Marie's touch was subtle yet profound. She might not have been the head, but she was undoubtedly the heart, ensuring the seamless operation of a program that stood as a testament to the university's commitment to social betterment. Her diligence paved the way for the program to flourish, enabling it to nurture counselors who would go on to embody the program's ideals.

Marie's work establishing and administering the graduate program may not be chronicled in the public domain, but its significance cannot be overstated. She crafted a space where learning was synonymous with empowerment, where students were equipped to extend rehabilitation beyond the clinical, touching lives in a way that only those versed in humanity's complex tapestry can.

In a role often overshadowed by academic figureheads, Marie Kozik was indispensable. She was the linchpin that held the program together, the silent force that propelled it forward. The impact of her administrative insight—though not captured in the limelight—resonates through generations of counselors and the lives they have transformed. In the delicate balance of running a program that dealt with human fragility, Marie's role was not just administrative—it was foundational.

3.76 Leo Kuplinski
Student Center

In the heart of Scranton, within the walls where young minds flourished, Leo Joseph Kuplinski toiled quietly, a steward of order amidst the chaos of youthful exuberance. His days, filled with the hum of fluorescent lights and the scuff of shoes against linoleum, were a testament to the unsung heroes who keep the gears of institutions turning. The University of Scranton Student Center, a crossroads of academic and social paths, knew his steady hands well.

Leo's was a life woven into the fabric of a community that valued the sweat of its brow as much as the vigor of its intellect. His tenure in the Maintenance Department before a well-earned retirement was marked not by fanfare but by the quiet nod of respect from those who understood the dignity in maintaining the pillars upon which their ambitions rested.

1968 cast a long shadow over Leo's household, as it did over countless homes in Scranton. His son, a scion of the same institution where Leo served, traded his cap and gown for the olive drab of the U.S. Army Special Forces. Vietnam was more than a headline; it was a visceral tear in the fabric of the Kuplinski family tapestry. The war, a distant thunder, became an intimate storm in their lives.

Unsung Pillars of the University of Scranton

For Leo, a World War II veteran, the conflict was a cruel echo of his past. It was the unspoken tension at dinner tables, the subtext of every "How are you?" and the silent prayer in every church pew. In the American Legion halls and the Sacred Hearts Church Holy Name Society meetings, men like Leo found solace in shared experiences, a brotherhood forged in the crucible of different yet hauntingly similar wars.

The impact of Vietnam on families in Scranton—a city built on the bedrock of hard work and sacrifice—was profound. The community bore its sorrows with a stoic face yet whose heart bled privately with each letter from the front lines. Leo's face, lined with the passage of time and the weight of worry for his son, was, among many, a mirror of the collective anxiety gripping a nation, city, and father.

Leo passed in the winter of his life, a season of reflection and remembrance. He left behind a legacy of quiet service to his country and the grounds that nurtured the minds of the future. In the Sacred Hearts Church parish cemetery, where he rests, the echoes of a life lived in understated devotion linger. The soil of Scranton, enriched by the lives of its sons and daughters, holds not just the memory of Leo Joseph Kuplinski but the stories of a generation that knew the price of peace and the value of a day's work.

3.77 Stanley Lankowski
Library

Stanley Lankowski's story is a mosaic of quiet dedication, a testament to the unsung heroes who keep the world of academia turning. In the early 1970s, he was the custodian of knowledge at the University of Scranton library—where the rustle of turning pages and the soft footsteps among the stacks were the predominant sounds.

In a realm predominantly navigated by women, Stanley's presence was not one of contrast but of complement. He was a silent sentinel amid the rows of books, his role no less crucial than the librarians who cataloged and the students who sought enlightenment within the library's walls.

The era changed, yet Stanley's daily rituals remained constant. He was the one who ensured the books were shelved correctly after the echoes of inquiry had faded. When the morning light crept through the windows, it would find him dusting off the tomes of knowledge, his motions as familiar as the author's names on the spines.

Though the library was a female-dominated sphere, Stanley's interactions were marked by mutual respect and quiet camaraderie. He might not have been at the forefront of academic discussions. Still, his contribution was in preserving the

Unsung Pillars of the University of Scranton

sanctity and order of the place—a task he performed with a sense of pride that needed no acknowledgment.

Stanley's story is not found in records or accolades; it is written in the marginalia of the library's daily life. It's in the appreciation of a student who finds a book exactly where it's supposed to be, in the nod of acknowledgment from a passing librarian, in the seamless operation of an institution that serves as a beacon of learning.

In an environment where many seek recognition, Stanley found fulfillment in the quiet assurance that his work was the foundation upon which the pillars of education stood tall. He was a keeper of a tradition that values every cog in the machine, knowing that without him, the flow of knowledge might just stutter. And so, Stanley Lankowski was as much a part of the narrative in the hallowed halls of the University of Scranton library as the volumes lined the shelves.

Unsung Pillars of the University of Scranton

3.78 Alma Lewis
Cafeteria

Alma Lewis is a name not etched in the annals of any grand history yet indelibly marked in the collective memory of those who passed through the University of Scranton's cafeteria in the early 1970s. It was where the clatter of trays and the steam from hot dishes formed the backdrop to the thrum of youthful discourse and idealism.

She stood among her peers, a cadre of food service workers, who, like the mortar between bricks, held together the day-to-day life of the institution. They were the unseen engines of a mid-sized Catholic university, their labor a constant in a place of transience. For many students, Alma and her colleagues were fixtures, as enduring as the venerable buildings that dotted the campus.

The work, for Alma, was a tapestry of routine woven with threads of satisfaction. Each tray she filled, each spill she wiped, carried the weight of a service that went beyond mere sustenance. Yet, aspirations simmered beneath the surface; some dreamed of education for their children, others of businesses they might own. For its part, the university perceived them through a lens of utility, integral yet often overlooked.

Unsung Pillars of the University of Scranton

Tenure among these workers varied as much as their backgrounds. Some, like Alma, were long-term sentinels of the serving line, while others were merely passing through, their stay at the university as brief as the seasons. Despite the ephemeral nature of some, a sense of camaraderie bound them, a solidarity born of shared labor.

Did they feel valued? In the churn of academia, recognition was often scarce. They were the quiet contributors to a student's day, their worth measured in the fullness of stomachs and the cleanliness of the dining space. Yet, they, too, yearned for acknowledgment, for the understanding that their work was more than a transaction and a vital thread in the fabric of university life.

What would have been a better way to work with them? Engagement, perhaps. An understanding that their hands, which dealt with the daily bread, were as crucial as the hands that penned the scholarly articles. Inclusion in the larger narrative of the university, recognition of their names and stories, and a seat at the table where decisions were made—these would have been steps toward a more holistic embrace of the likes of Alma Lewis, whose legacy is not written in records but in the lived experience of those she served.

Unsung Pillars of the University of Scranton

3.79 Katherine Lopatka
Cafeteria

In the warm embrace of the University of Scranton's cafeteria, amidst the clatter of trays and the murmur of young minds, there toiled a quiet sentinel of the hearth—Katherine Lopatka. She stood as one among the unsung, whose hands were as much a part of nurturing the future as the professors in the lecture halls. For Katherine, the cafeteria was more than a place of employment; it was a patchwork of her dedication to family, an extension of her kitchen at home.

The early 1970s were a time of transformation. Yet, some things remained steadfast—the importance of family and the need for both spouses to work for a middle-class dream, especially in the modest neighborhoods that skirted the university. Women like Katherine, who hailed from these humble beginnings, found strength in their dual roles. Their work was not merely a job; it was a piece of a larger struggle, a daily testament to their resilience and commitment to the ones they loved.

Katherine's routine, though not documented, can be imagined as a reflection of the times. She would rise with the sun, her day beginning long before the first student stumbled into the cafeteria for a morning coffee. Her hands, I envision, would have been quick and efficient, serving meals, offering smiles that hinted at a maternal warmth—quietly fortifying the next generation.

Unsung Pillars of the University of Scranton

After hours spent on her feet, she would return to her nest, where the second shift began. The fragrance of home-cooked meals would soon fill her residence; laundry would be tended to with a steady rhythm, and the laughter and needs of her children would envelop her evening. In the confines of her home, she was more than a cafeteria worker; she was the cornerstone of her family, a matriarch steering her kin through the ebbs and flows of life.

We may never truly know the intricacies of Katherine's story, but in the absence of records, we can surmise that her life was a tapestry woven with threads of sacrifice, love, and the quiet dignity of hard work. The women of her time, who juggled the demands of a job and family, were the unsung builders of their communities. Their legacy is measured not in accolades but in the lives they shaped, both at home and beyond their front doors. In her unassuming way, Katherine was a beacon of that enduring spirit.

3.80 Alice Loughman
Cafeteria

Alice Loughman, a woman of remarkable fortitude, once walked in the fabric of Scranton, where history lingers in the avenues and alleyways. At the University of Scranton's cafeteria, she was the assistant manager, a role she performed with an almost invisible elegance during the bustling early 1970s. The place, alive with the energy of academia, saw Alice as the conductor of a daily symphony, managing the ebb and flow of hungry students with a poise that made the hard work seem effortless.

Her life was a rich mosaic, with each piece representing her dedication to her family and community. As a homemaker, she had been the heart of her household, creating a nurturing environment for her two children. This nurturing nature extended to her professional life when she joined ARA Foods, infusing care, and a personal touch into her role at the university cafeteria.

1976 brought a new chapter in Alice's life as she entered into marriage, weaving together the threads of companionship and love, adding to the fabric of her entire life. Her faith stood as a pillar, solid and unwavering, within the community of the Immaculate Conception Church. In her early years of education at Cathedral High School, she provided a foundation in intellect and character, which she carried forward into every aspect of her existence.

The University of Scranton honored her longstanding service with the Order of Pro Deo Et Universitate, recognizing her for her duties performed and her spirit of generosity and commitment evident to all. Yet, her true memorial lies in the fond remembrances of those she served and the affectionate tales in the corridors she once walked.

Alice's journey on this earth ceased in 2007, but her essence remains woven into the community she loved. Resting in Cathedral Cemetery, she continues to be a part of Scranton's story, her narrative one of devotion, service, and the quiet strength that endures in the memories of those who had the fortune to know her.

Unsung Pillars of the University of Scranton

Unsung Pillars of the University of Scranton

3.81 James Mack
Print Shop

In the fabric of a modest Pennsylvanian town, there's a weave, tightly knit, of stories and lives that together form a picture of dynamic spirit and familial commitment. At the center of this tapestry is a man whose hands have turned the gears of the printing press, a linchpin in the educational tapestry of the University of Scranton.

In the dawning years of the 1970s, the landscape of academia was a different hue; the echo of the typewriter was the heartbeat of administration, and the printing department stood as the backbone of college communication. Here, our man, a steward of the printed word, led a department charged with an essential yet Herculean task. His domain was ink and paper, where bulletins, exam papers, newsletters, and every conceivable document necessary to the lifeblood of a bustling mid-sized Catholic institution were born. The clatter of machines was his symphony, and precision his creed.

His days were steeped in the alchemy of transforming digital texts into tactile reality. He oversaw the careful orchestration of offset printing presses, the collating machines that gathered pages into reports, and the binding equipment that gave them spine. His was an era when cut-and-paste meant scissors and glue, and graphic design was a meticulous draft on a drawing board. His

Unsung Pillars of the University of Scranton

team, a crew as diverse as the courses offered, mirrored his dedication—committed to deadlines with a craftsmanship that bordered on the devout.

Beyond the mechanics of his daily toil, he was a custodian of memories, capturing the fleeting moments of college life on printed pages that would yellow with age but never fade in value. From first-year orientations to graduation days, his was the silent hand that recorded, in ink, the milestones of thousands.

2008 marked not just a professional zenith but a personal one, as he, the consummate family man, celebrated a milestone of love and partnership: a golden anniversary with his wife. Their dance of half a century was a testament to the enduring nature of commitment, mirroring the steadfastness he showed in his vocational life.

Now, at 90, his legacy is not merely in the documents he created but in the lives he touched, the students he indirectly guided, and the family he lovingly nurtured. The city of Dunmore doesn't just house a man but a chapter of its history, living, breathing, and still writing its story through the lives of his progeny and the enduring mark he left on the annals of education.

3.82 Catherine Malia
Treasurer's Office

In the treasurer's office of the University of Scranton, amidst the hustle of a mid-sized Catholic institution, Catherine Rose Malia carved her niche in the early 1970s. A graduate of Dunmore High School, Catherine brought to the University a blend of hometown sensibility and steadfast dedication, qualities essential for the meticulous work that awaited her daily.

As an employee in the treasurer's office, Catherine's days were steeped in the financial sinews that kept the University's heart beating. She was the quiet sentinel behind the scenes, ensuring that tuition payments were processed, balancing ledgers with the precision of a skilled artisan, and managing the flow of funds that sustained the academic programs. Her responsibilities stretched to the scholarships and bursaries, where she might have been the unseen hand that guided a struggling student through a financial maze to emerge with the gift of education secured.

This was before the digital revolution transformed the workplace when ledgers were physical, calculations were done by hand or on machines that clacked and dinged at the end of a row. Catherine's role was pivotal, for the treasurer's office was the financial stronghold, handling everything from payroll to budget allocations for departments expanding as the University grew.

Unsung Pillars of the University of Scranton

The early '70s were a period of change and growth for institutions like the University of Scranton. Federal and state educational grants were becoming more prevalent, and the treasurer's office was at the forefront, interpreting new financial landscapes, weaving through the complexities of regulatory changes, and ensuring compliance with financial reporting that was growing ever more intricate.

Amid her professional life, 1973 marked a personal milestone for Catherine as she embraced a new chapter in marriage. Balancing her professional duties with her personal life, she exemplified the era's emerging spirit of the independent woman—someone who managed to uphold responsibilities at work while nurturing the warmth of family life.

Catherine's story is not one of grandiose achievements broadcasted to the world but rather the essential narrative of a person who contributed steadfastly to the fabric of an institution that shaped minds and spirits. Her work in the treasurer's office was a tapestry of numbers and ledgers, of financial stewardship and the quiet pride of a job well done—a role that, while often overlooked, was crucial to the University's legacy during those transformative years.

3.83 Eugene Mahoney
Loyola Hall

In the heart of Scranton, amongst the bustle of eager minds and the ivy-draped walls of the University, there worked a man known simply as "Gears" to his friends and colleagues. Eugene Mahone was a name that perhaps not every student knew, but one that was as much a cornerstone of the University of Scranton's Loyola Hall as the bricks that made up its venerable structure.

For sixteen years, Gears was the maestro of maintenance, the foreman who kept the cogs of this institution turning smoothly. His domain was the physical heartbeat of Loyola Hall, ensuring that the lights flickered on without thought, that the heat whispered warmth during those biting Pennsylvania winters, and that every door hinge was greased to a silent perfection.

His work, often cloaked behind the scenes, was as critical as any lecture in those classrooms. In the early 70s, when technology was far less intrusive, the physical mechanics of a building required a knowing hand, a keen eye, and a responsive touch. Gears and his team were responsible for the physical well-being of the facilities, attending to the boilers, the electrical circuits, and the physical infrastructure that is the lifeblood of an educational institution. A blown fuse or a burst pipe could throw

Unsung Pillars of the University of Scranton

the day's schedule into disarray, but under his watchful eye, such disruptions were few and far between.

Loyola Hall and the University of Scranton, a mid-sized Catholic beacon of learning, comprised several thousand souls. In this context, Gears was a guardian, not just of the physical space, but of the routine and order that enables academic pursuit.

Recognition of his quiet dedication came in 1974 when the Pro Deo et Universitate award found its way into his hands, a testament to the years he devoted to the silent gears of the University's daily life.

Beyond the confines of his work, Gears was woven into the fabric of the wider community. His faith anchored him to Saint Ann's Monastery Church, his fellowship found camaraderie at the Columbus Club, and his passion for the outdoors saw him active in the Lackawanna County Federation of Sportsmen's Clubs. Each facet of his life spoke to a man deeply rooted in his beliefs, community, and love for the natural world.

In 1979, the cogs turned slightly slower, and the halls felt quieter as Gears departed this world. His legacy, however, remains etched not only in the maintenance logs of Loyola Hall but in the memories of those who knew him, worked with him, and learned in the shadow of his efforts.

Eugene Mahone's "Gears" rests now in the serene embrace of Saint Augustine's Cemetery, his story inscribed in the annals of the University of Scranton, a reminder that the smooth running of an institution is often the result of unsung heroes like him.

Unsung Pillars of the University of Scranton

3.84 Glynn Martino
Print Shop

In the heart of the University of Scranton's vibrant grounds, where faith and intellect intertwine, E. Glynn Martino's story unfolded quietly. As the 1970s brought change and progress to this mid-sized Catholic haven, she found her calling within the university's print shop walls.

E. Glynn was the architect behind the scenes, a typesetter of the highest order. Her fingers meticulously arranged the cold metal type for two decades and a year, transforming blank pages into vessels of knowledge. The print shop, filled with the scent of ink and paper, resonated with the clatter of her typesetting machines, a sound as constant and comforting as the turning of pages in the library next door.

Though woven through with the threads of an ordinary existence, her life was anything but. A matriarch in her own right, E. Glynn shared a 53-year journey with her husband, a partnership that ended with his passing in 2000. Her devotion to her faith never faltered; she was a steadfast figure at the Divine Mercy Parish in Minooka and a long-time member of the now-historic Saint Mary of Czestochowa church.

Her hands, which once set type with such precision, also crafted meals that were nothing short of divine—a testament to her membership in the Catholic Mother's Association and her role as a mother to three. Her cooking was a language of love, spoken in the universal dialect of flavor and care.

The earthly chapter of E. Glynn Martino concluded in 2011, but her essence remains indelible in the memories of those she touched. Her dedication to her craft, her family, and her faith lingers like the last notes of a favorite hymn. Now, she rests in the Saint Mary of Czestochowa Parish Cemetery in Greenwood, her spirit forever intertwined with the community that shaped much of her life's work. Here, beneath the sheltering sky, she lies in peace, her legacy as enduring as the words she once set to paper.

Unsung Pillars of the University of Scranton

3.85 John Maslany
Student Center

Every morning, as the first light of dawn crept over the University of Scranton, John Maslany would unlock the doors of the Student Center with a sense of quiet pride. He wasn't just a caretaker but a silent guardian of a world teeming with youthful dreams and aspirations. In his worn but neat uniform, John moved through the halls with a rhythm that echoed the heartbeat of the campus.

John's world was one of simple routines and complex characters. He knew every nook and cranny of the Student Center like the lines on his weathered hands. The early 1970s brought waves of change, and he witnessed it all from his unassuming vantage point. The vibrant protests, the passionate debates, the laughter, and the tears – the Student Center was a microcosm of a world in turmoil, and John was its steadfast observer.

His tools were simple – a mop, a broom, a set of keys – but they were instruments of care to John. He treated the building not just as a structure of bricks and mortar but as a living, breathing entity that nurtured the hopes of tomorrow's leaders. The students might not have noticed him much, but he caught them. He saw their struggles and triumphs, often reflecting on his youth, a time of fewer complexities but similar hopes.

Unsung Pillars of the University of Scranton

John's work was more than maintenance; it was a form of stewardship. He believed in the sanctity of his duties, understanding that every swept floor and polished surface contributed to improving the students' environment. It wasn't just about keeping things clean; it was about preserving a space where minds could flourish without the distraction of disorder.

In the quiet hours of his shift, when the echoes of daytime activities had faded, John would sometimes pause and look around. He felt a deep connection to this place, a sense of belonging that transcended the physicality of his work. The Student Center, with its ever-changing faces and constant buzz of activity, was a testament to the enduring spirit of inquiry and growth. John was a silent participant in this dance of life, a custodian not just of a building but of a chapter in the lives of those who passed through its doors.

As John locked up the Student Center each night, he did so with quiet satisfaction, knowing that, in his humble way, he was contributing to something larger than himself. The job was not just a means to an end; it was a fulfilling journey, a silent witness to the tapestry of human experience woven daily within the walls he so diligently cared for.

Unsung Pillars of the University of Scranton

3.86 Agnes Mayer
Residence Halls

In the early 1970s, nestled in the hills of Scranton, Pennsylvania, stood a mid-size Catholic university, a beacon of higher learning for several thousand souls seeking education and enlightenment. Amid the red-brick buildings and manicured lawns, a different kind of nurturing took place, one less noticed but just as essential to the institution's lifeblood.

Enter the world of Agnes Mayer, a woman whose hands shaped the lived-in corners of the residence halls, turning chaos into order, soot into shine. She was part of the unseen cadre, the domestics, whose labor was as routine as it was vital. In those days, the domestic job in a Catholic university was not just about the scrub and polish; it was a silent vow to support a community's growth.

Who would apply for such a position, one might ask? Often, the unsung locals, sometimes immigrants, saw a semblance of security in the university's steady demand. They were mothers, wives, and occasionally single women, for whom this work meant survival, a means to feed their children, to keep a roof over their heads. The compensation was modest, often minimum wage, with few benefits. Yet, it was an honest earning when jobs were scarce, and the economy was unforgiving.

Unsung Pillars of the University of Scranton

In the community, such work was met with a duality of respect and invisibility. There was an unspoken honor in labor, especially in a town built on the backs of coal miners and railroad workers. Yet, domestics like Agnes often faded into the background, their stories untold, their struggles unnoticed by those whose lives they so intimately touched.

Did Agnes find satisfaction in her work? It's a question that hangs in the air, elusive as the dust motes she chased with her duster. Perhaps there was pride in the gleam of a freshly mopped floor, a comfort in the routine, a camaraderie amongst peers who understood the language of toil. Or maybe it was just a job, a means to an end, appreciated but not fulfilling in the way dreamers hope.

Some domestics made a career within the university walls, their years of service outlasting even professors' tenure. Others moved on, seeking different paths or perhaps the same work in different places. For Agnes, we cannot say for sure—like many of her stations, her story is etched not in stone but in the transient hearts of those she served.

In the early '70s, Scranton was a city grappling with change, its coal-streaked past giving way to a new era. Agnes and her fellow domestics were part of that transition, their labor a bridge from the old world to the new, their lives a testament to the quiet endurance often the most valid measure of a community's strength.

Unsung Pillars of the University of Scranton

3.87 John McCrone
Student Center

In the early 1970s, amidst the academic buzz of the University of Scranton, there was a man who played a crucial, yet often unnoticed, role in the daily life of the campus. His name was John McCrone, and he was a custodian of the student center, a place bustling with the energy and aspirations of young minds.

John's days began as a quiet sentinel in the predawn hours. While the rest of the campus lay in slumber, he was already hard at work, his mop moving in graceful arcs across the floor, his hands carefully wiping down surfaces, ensuring every corner of the student center was pristine for the day ahead. The rhythm of his work was like a heartbeat, steady and essential.

For John, this work was more than a job; it was a silent service to the community he held dear. He took pride in the gleaming floors and spotless windows, seeing them as his contribution to the vibrant life of the university. Under his watchful care, the student center was not just a building but a living, breathing space where ideas flourished and friendships blossomed.

Behind his quiet demeanor, John harbored dreams and reflections of his own. Sitting on an unassuming chair in the corner of the center during brief moments of rest, he would gaze out at the students, lost in thought. Perhaps he imagined a

Unsung Pillars of the University of Scranton

different path where circumstances might have led him to be one of the educators or scholars who roamed these halls. But these thoughts were transient visitors; he always returned to his duties with a renewed sense of purpose.

John's interactions with the students were fleeting yet meaningful. A nod here, a smile there — he was a familiar, reassuring presence in their collegiate journey. He witnessed the ebb and flow of student life, the changing faces and seasons, each leaving an indelible mark on his heart and the fabric of the university.

In John McCrone's story, there was a quiet dignity, a testament to the often overlooked yet vital contributions of individuals like him. His work in the student center was a silent orchestra that played a crucial part in the symphony of campus life. As he locked the doors each evening and the echo of his footsteps faded into the night, the legacy of his dedication remained, woven into the history of the University of Scranton, a narrative of unsung devotion and humble pride.

Unsung Pillars of the University of Scranton

3.88 Dale McElroy
Athletics

Dale McElroy's story isn't one spun from the usual yarn. With a mind for numbers and a heart for the game, this fellow carved a niche at the University of Scranton that few could dream of, let alone fill. An accounting graduate, he had the sort of understanding of balance that transcended ledgers and balance sheets, finding its true calling in the poise and recovery of athletes.

Though his tenure at the University began in '67, his roots in athletic healing ran back to times spent patching up sailors at the Naval Academy. McElroy, the man with hands as adept with tape and ice packs as they were with calculators and tax forms, was the inaugural bearer of the title' Athletic Trainer' at the University. His six years in that role were a testament to adaptation, commitment, and an earnest dedication to the well-being of those under his wing.

The '70s brought change, as they did for many, and McElroy, it was the onset of a new rule: the master's decree. Though his expertise was undeniable, academia's red tape saw him depart from the role that he had shaped and that had shaped him. Yet, even as he stepped into the corporate world, his legacy at the University remained unblemished, preserved in the ligaments and bones of every athlete he tended to.

Unsung Pillars of the University of Scranton

His brief stint as a golf coach might seem a footnote, but for those seasons, the greens and fairways of Scranton knew the tread of a man who was more than a trainer; he was a mentor. Under his watch, the golf team soared to a conference victory that still echoes in the halls of the University.

Behind the accolades and achievements was a man who lived for the game and its players. His life, marked by the early loss of his beloved wife, was a portrait of resilience—a quality he imparted to every athlete he encountered. McElroy, a man of firsts for the University, left a legacy more about the lives he touched than the records he set.

And so, the story of Dale McElroy is one of quiet heroism that found its stage not in the roar of a crowd at a championship game but in the serene gratitude of athletes who knew they had someone in their corner, in the truest sense of the word.

Unsung Pillars of the University of Scranton

3.89 Mary McGloin
Cafeteria

Mary's story is a woven patchwork of the everyday and the remarkable threads of the mundane and the extraordinary interlaced in the fabric of her life. In the bustling corridors and the steam-clouded confines of the University of Scranton's cafeteria, Mary Mies McGloin served not just meals but moments of respite, her smile a familiar comfort to many students and staff.

Mary was a constant amid the clatter of cutlery and the chatter of diners, an employee of ARA Services, the company that fed the university's lifeblood. Her work, often unseen and unsung by many, was the bedrock of daily life in the cafeteria, her dedication as unwavering as the daily menu.

The early '70s brought both the hum of her workday and the silence of personal loss, with her husband's passing leaving echoes in the halls of her heart. But Mary's resilience was steadfast and reliable as the sturdy tables she wiped down. Her education, gleaned from the city schools of Scranton, had instilled in her a quiet wisdom and a profound sense of community that she carried like a diploma.

Retirement in '83 was a punctuation, not an end, as the Women of the University of Scranton gathered to celebrate her—not for her service alone but for her spirit, which had nourished them in ways beyond the physical. Two years later, Mary's chapter closed in the same pages of Scranton that had chronicled her entire tale.

Mary's legacy, carried on by a son and a daughter, lies not in the grand gestures but in the remembered kindnesses and the shared laughter amidst the daily grind. She rests now in Cathedral Cemetery, her story etched in the memories of those she touched, a testament to a life that, in its simplicity, was profoundly meaningful.

Unsung Pillars of the University of Scranton

3.90 Cynthia McKnight
Registrar's Office

Cynthia McKnight's tale is woven from the fabric of routine, a thread in the vast tapestry of academia. In the Registrar's Office at the University of Scranton, a mid-sized Catholic college in the early 1970s, her days were a steady cadence of records and requisitions.

Picture this: when computers were novelties, and data lived in towering metal file cabinets. The Registrar's Office was the nerve center of the university, a place where the pulse of student progress was meticulously monitored. Employees like Cynthia were the custodians of student records, from admission to graduation and everything in between.

Their training? It's not formal, in the way we think of it now. It was on-the-job, a learning-by-doing in an era when experience trumped credentials. They were skilled in the art of organization, adept at deciphering handwritten forms, and fluent in the language of academic regulations. Precision was their mantra; confidentiality was their creed.

Were they well-paid? Not particularly. Appreciated? In quiet ways, perhaps, by the student whose record they corrected, by the faculty member whose class list they updated. But theirs was not a work of glory. It was the work of the groundwork, the unseen foundation upon which the academic year was built.

As for aspirations, they varied as much as the individuals themselves. Some, like Cynthia, may have yearned for more - a rise through the administrative ranks, a chance to shape policy rather than enforce it. Others found satisfaction in the order they brought to chaos and pride in a well-done job.

The Registrar's Office was an ecosystem of paper and protocol, and Cynthia McKnight was a steward of its legacy. Her unverifiable but imaginable story is a reminder of the countless unseen hands that keep the wheels of institutions turning.

Unsung Pillars of the University of Scranton

3.91 Rose Mecca
Residence Halls

Rose Mecca's story is woven into the fabric of a town steeped in the virtues of hard work and close-knit community values. Born in 1914 into the bustling life of Scranton, Pennsylvania, Rose's tale is one of quiet resilience and unspoken fortitude. Scranton's public schools had been her alma mater, a foundation that would hold her in good stead throughout the trials and tribulations of life as modest as it was meaningful.

When her hands weren't busy tending to the needs of the residence halls at the University of Scranton, you could find Rose immersed in the life of Dunmore. After a long day's work in this municipality, many university employees laid their heads. Dunmore was not just a place on a map; it was a testament to a collective ethos, where the word 'neighbor' still held weight, and a person's worth was measured by the sweat of their brow and the strength of their phrase.

For 50 years, this was Rose's world. She'd watched it change and stay the same, where the coal dust of yesteryear had settled into a communal spirit of grit and grace. It was here that she and her husband, a man she bid farewell to just a year before her departure, shared a life, raised three sons, and etched their legacies into the heartbeats of those they knew.

Unsung Pillars of the University of Scranton

Rose's story is not one of grandeur or headlines. It's etched in the quiet corners of the University of Scranton, in the well-worn steps of the residence halls she cared for, halls that echoed with the laughter of generations of students. Her legacy is carried on in the lives of her sons, the very embodiment of the work ethic she personified.

When Rose retired, she left behind more than just a mop and a bucket; she left behind the echoes of a time when service was a noble calling. Her final resting place lies in the Italian-American Cemetery, among the marble headstones that stand as silent custodians of the Italian-American narrative in Scranton. In the hallowed earth, Rose Mecca's story finds its quietus here, her spirit interwoven with the very soil of the city she helped to build, one day's labor at a time.

3.92 Joseph Metzger
Cafeteria

In the heart of the University of Scranton, a place steeped in tradition and faith, there was a corner where the aroma of coffee mingled with the scent of freshly baked bread and the sounds of young minds engaging in the latest debates. This corner, the university cafeteria, was more than a place of sustenance; it was a hub of community and conversation. It was the early 1970s, an era of change and challenge, and amidst this, the cafeteria stood as a testament to constancy and comfort.

Enter Joseph Metzger, a man whose hands were as accustomed to the heft of a spoon as they once were to the handle of a hammer. His presence in the cafeteria was a statement in itself. Here was a man, amongst a minority of men in the food service staff, who brought the echoes of industries that once thrummed with vigor - factories, railroads, and mines.

Metzger's journey to the cafeteria was not charted by youthful aspiration but by the necessity of changing times. The industries that once defined the landscape of Scranton were fading, and men like him sought refuge in the warm embrace of the university's hearth. This transition, this second act in their working lives, was facilitated by ARA Services, a contractor that managed the cafeteria's operations. They offered a new start, albeit starkly different from the soot and sweat of a factory floor.

Unsung Pillars of the University of Scranton

ARA Services, a name that resonated with corporate efficiency, was adept at running such facilities. They managed the logistics, the supplies, and the menus, turning the university's need for a dining service into a smoothly running operation. Yet, within this systematized structure, employees like Metzger found a space to weave the fabric of their dignity and work ethic into their new roles.

The presence of men like Metzger in the cafeteria was a gentle ripple in the pond. They were the minority in a domain traditionally staffed by women, yet their contribution was substantial. This shift from physical labor's ruggedness to service's subtleties wasn't always comfortable. Their aspirations were humble: a steady job, a kind word, a nod of appreciation from those they served. But they brought a sense of camaraderie and resilience that enriched the atmosphere.

In the cafeteria, under the watchful care of ARA and the stewardship of employees like Metzger, students found nourishment for the body and soul. The cafeteria was where the past met the present, where the stories of a changing America were shared over plates of food. It was where Metzger and his colleagues, who once fueled the engines of America's industry, found a new purpose. They became the unseen pillars of a community, serving not just food but offering a daily reminder of the dignity of all work, the strength of adaptation, and the enduring spirit of the human heart.

3.93 Joseph Michalik
Saint Thomas Hall

In the corridors of Saint Thomas Hall, the heart of the University of Scranton, there was a hum, a rhythmic beat that sustained the institution's life. It was more than the murmur of studious youth or the echo of scholarly lectures. It was the sound of maintenance, the backdrop of academia in the early 1970s. And Joseph Michalik was a silent maestro in this realm of unsung labor.

Michalik, a figure now blurred by time's unforgiving passage, was a man of routine. Each morning, as the sun peeked over the Pocono Mountains, his day would begin with the jingle of a heavy key ring and the clanking of a toolbox. His realm was the behind-the-scenes, the boiler rooms and the back corridors, the places glossed over by the glossy brochures of the university.

To understand the role of a maintenance worker like Michalik in a mid-sized Catholic university at this time is to understand a world of unseen gears. These men ensured that the heat whispered through the vents during frigid Pennsylvania winters and that the lights flickered to life in the dim chapels and crowded libraries. Their work was essential, yet it went largely unnoticed; their presence was felt only in the smooth operation of campus life.

Unsung Pillars of the University of Scranton

Maintenance operation at such an institution was a tapestry of tasks, each thread as crucial as the next. The early '70s lacked the digital management systems that orchestrated modern maintenance endeavors. Instead, there were logbooks, dog-eared and coffee-stained, where requests were scribbled and schedules penned. Men like Michalik would report to a supervisor, receiving assignments ranging from the mundane—fixing a leaky faucet—to the urgent—restoring heat to a dormitory.

For these men, predominantly middle-aged and carrying the weight of their experiences in factories, railroads, and mines, the university was a stark contrast to their previous workplaces. It was cleaner, safer, and perhaps less physically demanding, but came with challenges. These were men whose hands had known the roughness of coal and the heat of the foundry, now tasked with the delicate preservation of a place of learning.

Their aspirations were varied. Some sought the stability of the job and its benefits for their families. Others, like whispers, harbored dreams of something more, perhaps inspired by the thrum of youthful ambition surrounding them. Yet, they found comfort in their roles and pride in their contribution to the greater good of the institution. It was a position that, while not glamorous, offered dignity in service and camaraderie in shared purpose.

In the end, the story of Joseph Michalik and his peers is not one of individual glory but rather a collective narrative of dedication. It is a tribute to the men whose workday was punctuated by the tolling of the campus bell, marking hours not in achievements or accolades but in tasks completed and crises averted. They were the quiet keepers of the university's heartbeat, a pulse that ensured the future could be written in the classrooms above.

Unsung Pillars of the University of Scranton

3.94 Harold Miles
Long Center

In the heart of Scranton, within the sturdy walls of the University's Long Center, Harold Miles walked the echoing corridors with a ring of keys jangling at his belt, a symphony of metal that announced his approach. To the untrained eye, Harold was merely a custodian, another cog in the institution's day-to-day operation machine. But to those who saw, he was as vital as the beams holding the building.

Harold came to the University after the coal mines closed when the dust had settled, and men like him sought refuge in the stability of maintenance work. The Athletic Center was his domain, where young ambitions burned bright, and sweat was a testament to perseverance. As a maintenance man, Harold was tasked with the upkeep of the sprawling facilities: the polished gleam of the basketball court, the measured lines of the track, and the chlorinated blue of the swimming pool. He repaired lockers, attended to the squeals and complaints of aging equipment, and ensured the lights shone down on each game like spotlights on a stage.

The operation was meticulous, a carefully orchestrated dance between man and machine. Each morning, Harold and his team divided the tasks with military precision. The clink of tools and the hiss of a steam pipe were the sounds of progress, of things being set to right under Harold's watchful eye.

The University was a haven for Harold and his peers, middle-aged men who'd known the factories' grit, the railroads' grime, or the mines' dark embrace. It was a place of respectability and quiet dignity, where their knowledge of things that worked, moved, and needed fixing found a new purpose. They took pride in their work, even as their hands, rough from years of labor, turned valves and twisted wrenches.

Yet, within Harold's chest beat the heart of aspiration. This job, dignified and essential as it was, might have been a rest stop on a road not taken. There was a sense of comfort in the routine and a whisper of 'what if?'—a question that lingered in the locker rooms long after the athletes had gone home.

Maintenance work in a mid-sized Catholic institution in the early 1970s was not just about keeping the lights on; it was about maintaining a legacy, a tradition and ensuring that the hallowed halls where future leaders, thinkers, and doers were being molded remained a testament to the sanctity of education and the pursuit of excellence.

Harold, with his keys and his quiet ways, understood this. He wasn't just maintaining the Long Center; he was preserving a future he believed in, even if it was one he would only ever brush with calloused hands.

Unsung Pillars of the University of Scranton

3.95 Grace Miller
Advanced Study Advisory Office

Grace Miller's days at the University of Scranton began in the late '60s, an era of change that echoed through academia just as it did on the streets. In 1969, the university was a microcosm of the larger world, brimming with the tension and excitement of transformation. With her sharp eye for detail and a heart as big as the Pennsylvania sky, Grace stepped into this world not as a scholar but as a staffer, her hands destined to shape futures rather than pen treatises.

Her first role was clerical, a position that often goes unnoticed, the gears in the tremendous academic machine. But Grace was not one to be overshadowed by the humdrum of administration. By 1974, her presence and prowess had earned her a promotion to Assistant Director of Career Services. This title came with a weighty responsibility: to be a beacon for those adrift in the sea of academic and professional choices.

In a time when the expectation of gender often accompanied the ink on diplomas, Grace's rise to a position of such influence without a college degree was a testament to her exceptional ability. It was a nod, subtle yet significant, from the university's old guard to the winds of change.

Unsung Pillars of the University of Scranton

As the institution shifted from its all-male legacy to a coeducational bastion, Grace stood at the helm of this transition, witnessing and actively forging the path for the women walking the campus paths after her. Yes, she was a part of the career services. Still, more so, she was a career service herself—a lifeline to students and alums alike, offering guidance as they navigated the crossroads of education and ambition.

Her office became a sanctuary where dreams were given direction. Grace's advice, always served with a side of Scranton warmth, wasn't just about resumes and interviews; it was about the courage to leap, the resolve to pursue advanced studies, and the strength to carve out a space in the professional world.

Away from the university, Grace's life was equally filled with service and community. The Faculty guild knew her as a force, a voice that championed the cause of her peers. The Scranton Prep Mothers Club bore witness to her dedication to education, not just within the hallowed university grounds but in nurturing young minds preparing to step into those halls.

At home, in the heart of Scranton, her two children grew up with the university as a backdrop, a place that was as much a part of their lives as their mother's. The spark of Grace's trailblazing spirit flickered brightly in them, a legacy in its own right.

By her very essence, Grace Miller embodied the change she helped usher in at the University of Scranton. In her story, we find the quiet strength of a woman who didn't just do her job but lived it, touching countless futures with the wisdom of her presence. Her path was not laid with the mortarboard and gown but with an unwavering commitment to service, an inspiring chapter in the university's history.

3.96 Estelle Misorek
Computer Center

In the early 1970s, tucked away in the heart of the University of Scranton, a revolution was quietly taking place amidst the hum of massive computers. It was a time when these machines began to redefine academia when punch cards were the keys to unlocking vast stores of knowledge. In the middle of this technological transformation was Estelle Misorek, a name not widely known yet whose story is etched in the memory of those colossal computing rooms.

Estelle, a sharp and determined employee at the University Computer Center, was part of a pioneering group that operated and understood the complex mainframes. The computers of that era were behemoths—IBM systems that filled rooms, their data stored on reels of magnetic tape, and input through cards with holes punched by hand. For students, these machines were a marvel, a gateway to new research and statistical analysis that were previously unfathomable.

In those days, computing was not just a skill but a craft that required patience and precision. Like many women in the field then, Estelle found herself in a domain dominated by men. Yet, she and her female colleagues were not mere observers but integral to running these computer centers. They learned on the job, through manuals thick as city directories, and by exchanging knowledge amongst peers.

The role of women like Estelle was multifaceted—they were operators, programmers, and sometimes, educators. They were the translators between the rigid language of the computers and the inquiring minds of students and faculty. They were not always in the spotlight, and their contributions were often overshadowed by their male counterparts. Still, they were the backbone of the operation, ensuring that these mystifying machines performed as needed.

As for appreciation, it came quietly and without fanfare. Their legacy, however, is profound. They were the trailblazers for the generations of women to go in the computing field, setting the stage for a future where gender became less a barrier and more a bridge to innovation.

Today, when we look back at the evolution of technology and education, we must remember the Estelles of the world. They may not have headlines in history books, but their meticulous work and dedication laid the groundwork for the digital age we seamlessly navigate today. Their story is a testament to women's quiet strength and critical role in advancing technology and education.

3.97 Mary Mitchell
Residence Halls

In the heart of a mid-level Catholic university, where the bricks bore the weight of tradition and the halls echoed with the ambitions of its youthful occupants, the residence halls stood as silent witnesses to the transformation of generations. It was here, in the early 1970s at the University of Scranton, that Mary Mitchell, whose story is much like a thread woven through the fabric of this institution, played her part behind the scenes.

Mary's days would begin as the dawn barely broke over the Scranton skyline, the chill of the Pennsylvania morning as constant as her presence. As a domestic in the University Residence Halls, her role was pivotal, yet often unnoticed by those whose lives she indirectly touched. The clink of her keys and the soft shuffle of her footsteps through the carpeted corridors marked the rhythm of a day's hard work.

In those halls, the air was heavy with the scent of polish and disinfectant, signs of Mary's diligence. She was part of a team that ensured the cleanliness and orderliness of the students' living quarters. From scrubbing bathrooms to changing linens, the domestic staff's tasks were as essential as they were endless. Their hands erased the remnants of youthful revelry and maintained an environment conducive to learning and personal growth.

Unsung Pillars of the University of Scranton

The students, absorbed in their studies and social lives, may have only offered a fleeting smile or a casual 'thank you' as they passed Mary in the hallways. The recognition of her labor was not measured in accolades but in the seamless continuity of daily life within the residence halls. Their modest compensation reflected the times and undervaluing of such vital work.

Yet, Mary and her colleagues were educators in their own right. Through their work ethic and interactions, they imparted lessons on respect, responsibility, and the dignity of labor. They were models of a work ethic many students had not encountered closely before. The domestic staff showed that every role in a community, no matter how behind-the-scenes, contributes to the greater whole.

Their legacy is not etched in the stone of the buildings they kept or the awards they never received, but rather in the lived experience of the students who, perhaps later in life, realized the value of the work done by people like Mary. The young men and women who left those halls became leaders, thinkers, and doers, carrying the academic lessons of their professors and the unspoken teachings of the domestic staff who made their daily lives possible.

To appreciate Mary's legacy is to understand that the heart of an educational institution beats not just in its classrooms but also in the quiet corridors where people like her worked tirelessly, ensuring the wheel of education turned without hindrance. In the University of Scranton story, Mary Mitchell is a silent yet enduring character, representing the many unsung individuals who have contributed to shaping minds and spirits in the embrace of those hallowed halls.

Unsung Pillars of the University of Scranton

3.98 Donna Moffitt
Bookstore

In the heart of a bustling mid-level Catholic university in the early 1970s, nestled among the brick-laden paths and ivy-covered walls, the University of Scranton's bookstore was a beacon of knowledge and resource. Donna Moffitt, a name that might not echo through the halls of academia but is etched in the memories of those who frequented the campus bookstore, was a linchpin in this haven of academia.

Donna's days were woven into the fabric of university life, a tapestry of textbooks, conversation, and the quiet hum of fluorescent lights. She was the custodian of knowledge, overseeing rows upon rows of books that were more than mere commodities—they were passports to learning, to futures yet written. Her role transcended that of a mere cashier or stocker; she was an unsung academic facilitator whose recommendations often guided the course of a student's scholarly pursuits.

The bookstore operated like a well-oiled machine, with each cog—each staff member—playing a crucial role in the education of students. They were advisors, knowledgeable about the texts and materials that formed the backbone of the university's curriculum. The staff, often students themselves, were a bridge between the academic departments and the pupils, decoding

Unsung Pillars of the University of Scranton

professors' syllabi and ensuring the suitable materials were in the right hands.

Compensation for this role was modest. It was a time before barcodes and digital inventories, where every book logged, and every transaction made was by hand, a testament to the meticulous nature of the job. The hours were long, and the work was demanding, but there was a camaraderie in shared purpose and struggles. Respect for their work varied; some saw them as essential, others as mere transaction facilitators. But to the discerning eye, their contribution was invaluable.

Their legacy is not in the books sold or the supplies distributed but in their unquantifiable impact on the student body. They were the background players in the grand play of education, seldom spotlighted but always present. As alums return to campus, they may not remember Donna Moffitt by name, but they will remember the bookstore, where their educational journey took shape, and they will feel the echoes of the staff's dedication.

The legacy of Donna and her colleagues is found in the quiet success of generations of students who passed through the university, each carrying a piece of wisdom imparted, intentionally or not, by the guardians of the university bookstore.

Unsung Pillars of the University of Scranton

3.99 Joseph Moffitt
Long Center

Joseph Moffitt was the steady pulse in the Long Center in the rhythmic heart of the University of Scranton amidst the echoes of bouncing basketballs and the sharp scent of polished hardwood. This athletic facility was his charge. As he was known by staff and students alike, Joe served not just as the superintendent but as the soul of the place. His domain was one of sweat and ambition, where young athletes sought to surpass their limits.

Joe's days were a tapestry woven from myriad threads— maintaining the grandeur of the courts, ensuring the locker rooms were sanctuaries of solace and preparation, and that every scoreboard lit up with the promise of the next big game. He was the first to arrive, his mornings starting with the hum of fluorescent lights and often the last to leave, his evenings ending with the click of locks and the dimming of those same lights.

His challenges were as diverse as the events the Long Center hosted. The wear of time on the building, the constant need for repairs and updates, the balancing act between budget constraints, and the aspirations of a university swelling with pride were the weights he lifted daily. Yet, he carried them as the athletes had their own—steadfastly, without complaint.

Unsung Pillars of the University of Scranton

The social fabric of the campus was one he was intricately woven into. Joe wasn't just a staff member but a fixture, as much a part of the university's identity as the crest emblazoned on its flags. He didn't command respect through his title but earned it through his dedication. The students might not have known the depth of his responsibilities, but they knew the man who gave them a nod of encouragement, slipped into the stands to watch a game, and beamed with pride at each victory, however small.

His fulfillment didn't come from accolades or public recognition; it came from the seamless execution of a tournament, the laughter of students free from the weight of their studies, and the comfort of knowing he played his part in their journey. And when tragedy struck, snatching him from the world in 1975, the silence in the Long Center was palpable, a testament to the space he occupied in life.

Joseph Moffitt, a Scranton native, left a legacy in bricks and mortar and the hearts of those he touched. A family man, survived by a wife, four daughters, and two sons, he was laid to rest in Cathedral Cemetery, leaving behind a community that had become his extended family. They grieved not just for the man but for the quiet strength, the unseen hand that had guided so many of their days.

His life spoke quietly but resonated deeply, a reminder that fulfillment often lies not in the light of recognition but in the shadows of unassuming service.

Unsung Pillars of the University of Scranton

3.100 Joseph Moreno
Cafeteria

In the heart of the University of Scranton, where the echo of youthful aspirations and the scent of history intertwine, Joseph Moreno spent his days amidst the clatter of cutlery and the buzz of student chatter. An employee of the food service contractor ARA, Joseph was a fixture in the university cafeteria, a silent guardian of sustenance.

His days began before dawn, the first to unlock the doors to a day's promise of nourishment. As students trickled in, drawn by the wafting aroma of fresh coffee and baked bread, Joseph was there, a steady hand amidst the flurry of breakfast rushes. His responsibilities were manifold: overseeing the inventory, ensuring each dish that left the kitchen met the unwritten standards of both health and taste, managing staff who looked to him for direction, and perhaps most daunting, catering to the capricious tastes of a thousand young scholars.

The challenges were as constant as the seasons. The balance between cost and quality was a tightrope walk, and food waste was a specter that haunted the margins. Yet, Joseph faced these with a resolve that spoke of a deep commitment to the job and the community he served.

Unsung Pillars of the University of Scranton

Joseph's position was unassuming yet indispensable in the social tapestry of campus life. His domain was the hearthstone of academia, where students and faculty gathered for a momentary reprieve from the rigors of intellectual pursuits. He was the unseen hand that fortified them for exams and celebrated with them their triumphs.

Did he feel appreciated? In the nods of satiated diners, the casual thanks tossed over shoulders, perhaps there was recognition. But in the proper fashion of those who work behind the scenes, Joseph's satisfaction was not in the accolades but in the smooth operation of the gears of daily life.

His legacy, unetched in plaques or statues, lives in the quieter annals of memory: in the alums who might return years later, finding comfort in the familiar scents of the cafeteria, in the traditions he helped maintain, and in the shared experiences of generations who passed through those doors. For Joseph Moreno, the University of Scranton was not just a workplace but a chapter in a larger story, one he penned daily with a spoon and a smile, leaving an indelible imprint on the canvas of countless lives.

Unsung Pillars of the University of Scranton

Unsung Pillars of the University of Scranton

3.101 Alice Murphy
Registrar's Office

Alice Murphy was a familiar fixture in a small, bustling office filled with the constant clatter of typewriters and the quiet hum of diligent academia. Her days at the University of Scranton were a symphony of schedules, a balancing act of appointments, and a continuous liaison between the energetic student body and the esteemed faculty. As the assistant to the dean of the College of Arts and Sciences in the early 1970s, Alice was the unseen ligament that held the college's academic muscles together.

The responsibility on Alice's shoulders was immense; she was the guardian of the dean's calendar, the orchestrator of faculty meetings, and the custodian of confidential records. Her challenges were manifold - from smoothing over the ruffled feathers of academia to ensuring that the dean's directives were disseminated with precision. She found fulfillment in the seamless execution of a well-organized conference and the quiet acknowledgment of a well-done job.

Alice's social standing on campus was akin to that of a silent sentinel. Known to all, yet cloaked in the modesty of her role, she was the heart of operations, pulsing quietly behind the scenes. She was just another staff member to the outside world, but she was indispensable to those who operated within the academic cloisters.

Appreciation, in Alice's experience, was a subtle currency. It came not in grand gestures but in the knowing nods across the hall, the brief smiles in the cafeteria, and the occasional "thank you" that held a world of meaning. Her gratification was in the success of the college's endeavors, in the knowledge that her silent contribution was vital.

Before her days at the university, Alice honed her skills at the Scranton Electric Company and the International Correspondence School, a testament to her adaptability and her commitment to professional growth. A graduate of Lackawanna Business College and Scranton Central High School, she embodied the spirit of her hometown - resilient, dynamic, and ever-forward-looking.

Alice Murphy, a wife and mother, managed to weave her family life into her demanding career seamlessly, a feat that spoke volumes of her organizational prowess and unwavering commitment to all facets of her life.

Her legacy lies not in a plaque or a building named in her honor but in the countless graduates who benefited from the smoothly run college she helped oversee, in the policies shaped by the dean's office, and in the precedence she set for professional women in a time of burgeoning gender equality. It is a legacy of quiet strength, resilience, and the enduring power of the unsung heroes that shape the future, one day at a time.

Unsung Pillars of the University of Scranton

3.102 James Murphy
Painter

James W. Murphy Jr. painted his life with broad and resilient strokes, much like the ones he used on the canvas of the University of Scranton's walls. Every day, amidst the bustle of academia, he was a constant, his painter's overalls as much a part of the university as the bricks and mortar he beautified.

His duties were straightforward but critical: maintain the aesthetic integrity of an institution that prides itself on appearance and intellect. The challenges? The relentless Northeastern weather, the occasional graffiti, the unforgiving nature of time that peeled away at his work like it did at all things. Yet, he painted on.

To students and faculty, James might have been a fleeting figure on a ladder against the backdrop of their daily lives, but to him, each stroke was a testament to his commitment to the community. In the grand tapestry of the university's life, he was a thread that might've seemed insignificant but was vital all the same.

His position, while not glamorous, was fulfilling in its own right. It offered him a canvas to contribute to the place that had shaped his early years, where he attended classes after serving his country with the same steadfast dedication. The University of

Unsung Pillars of the University of Scranton

Scranton wasn't just his employer; it was part of his identity, and in turn, he became part of its legacy.

Socially, he was a man of quiet dignity, his conversations perhaps not echoing in the halls of academia but resonating in the more hallowed halls of Saint Paul's church and the camaraderie with fellow veterans and Knights of Columbus members. He was respected, a man of few words but of reliable action.

Appreciation is a complex mural—often, the artist only gets a nod while the art is lauded. Did James feel appreciated? Perhaps in the smiles he earned for a job well done, in the nods of acknowledgment from professors who knew the value of a pristine environment for education, and in the quiet satisfaction of preserving the beauty of a place he held dear.

Retirement came with the honor of a craftsman who had served his union, community, and family with unwavering dedication. The brushstrokes ceased, but the colors he left behind remained vibrant in the memories of those who walked the university's corridors.

His legacy, much like the walls he painted, stands firm. It's in the hallowed halls of the University of Scranton, in the history of a small Pennsylvanian town, and in the hearts of a daughter and two sons who carry forward the story of a man who served his country, church, and community. James W. Murphy Jr., a Marine Corps veteran, a devoted church member, a loving husband and father, and the painter who left his mark in more ways than one, rests at Saint Catherine's cemetery, his life's portrait complete, his memory indelible.

3.103 Margaret Murrin
Dean of Arts and Sciences Office

Margaret Murrin's story unfolds in the hallowed halls of the University of Scranton, weaving through the corridors of academia, not as a heralded professor or a tenured dean but as the ligament that held the institution's fabric together. Her title, executive secretary for the academic dean, belies the magnitude of her role – she was a confidant to the educators, a navigator for the students, and a cornerstone of the administration.

Graduating from Scranton Technical High School, Margaret carried the pride of her local education as she further honed her skills at Lackawanna Business School. These institutions, steeped in the city's history, were the launchpad for a career dedicated to improving her community through education.

In the early 1970s, when Margaret's tenure at the University of Scranton began, she entered a world on the cusp of change. Her initial role in the counseling center was less about administrative tasks and more about understanding the zeitgeist of a student body navigating the tumult of the era. She was a listening ear, a discreet adviser, and often, the gentle nudge guiding students towards their potential.

Unsung Pillars of the University of Scranton

Later, as the executive secretary to the academic dean, Margaret's days were a ballet of orchestrated chaos: managing schedules, drafting correspondence, and being the unseen hand that smoothed the ripples of academic life. Her challenges were many - the delicate balance of academia's egos, the relentless pace of term cycles, and the ever-present need to innovate administrative processes.

Her social standing on campus was unique; she wasn't just staff – she was part of the university's essence. To the faculty, she was indispensable. She was their unspoken advocate to the students, and she was the right hand to the dean. Did she feel appreciated? In the quiet moments, when a crisis was averted or a student thanked her, there was a glimmer of recognition, but like many unsung heroes, her fulfillment came not from accolades but from the success of those she served.

Margaret's personal life bore its marks of resilience. She was a widower, having lost her husband in the 1990s, yet she carried on with a quiet strength that was both formidable and inspiring. Her love and pride for her daughter were profound, a beacon guiding her through darker moments.

Her faith was a constant, a lifelong devotion embodied by her membership at the Immaculate Conception church. She found solace, community, and the strength to serve others with a grace that was as much a part of her as her heartbeat.

Unsung Pillars of the University of Scranton

Margaret Murrin passed away in 2010, her final resting place among the whispering pines of Cathedral Cemetery, a testament to her deep roots in the Scranton community. Her legacy is not etched in the annals of academia nor chronicled in textbooks. It lives in the countless lives she touched, the students she set on the path to greatness, the faculty she supported, and the daughter who carries her spirit forward. It's a legacy of quiet service, unsung dedication, and the indelible mark one woman left on the heart of a university.

3.104 Randolph Myers
Library

In the heart of the University of Scranton, there was a man whose hands turned the cogs of the daily grind with quiet resilience. Randolph Myers, a name not emblazoned in history books but etched in the corridors of the university library, carried the torch of his duties with a stoic grace.

Randolph was the silent sentinel of the library's inner workings, a maintenance man by title but a custodian of legacy in spirit. Amidst the hushed whispers of students buried in their books, his boots echoed softly as he went about his rounds. Shelves dusted, floors swept, bulbs changed—a symphony of tasks executed meticulously.

His challenges were many, the fixes never-ending. A loose tile, a flickering light, the persistent hum of an air conditioner—all beckoning his attention. Yet, he took pride in these battles against entropy, for in every repair, he saw the maintenance of order and the facilitating of education.

Randolph's social standing on campus was not of an academic, yet he was an integral thread in the university fabric. His presence was constant, like the steady tick of a clock—often unnoticed but essential. To the students and faculty, he was a fixture as reliable as the books themselves, and in that reliability, he found fulfillment.

Appreciation is a currency often in short supply for those in service roles, but Randolph's satisfaction was drawn from the job's intrinsic rewards. His fulfillment didn't hinge on accolades but on the gleam of well-polished floors and the smooth operation of the library's daily life.

He had known a life of rigor and discipline as a World War II Army veteran. The Asiatic-Pacific Campaign and the harrowing experiences in Burma had shaped a man who understood the depth of freedom and the value of quiet service. His was not a path of grand recognition but one of personal triumphs and the peace of duty well done.

At the Bethel AME Church, he was more than a member; he was a trustee, a steward of faith and community. His service there was another testament to his commitment to support structures that uplifted others through spiritual guidance or the maintenance of the church's sanctity.

Ultimately, Randolph Myers rests in the serenity of Forest Hill Cemetery in Dunmore, his life's tale told by the tranquility of his final resting place.

His legacy? It lies in the unseen, the everyday, the ordinary turned extraordinary by dedication. It lives on in the smooth functioning of the library, in the hearts he touched, and in the quiet recognition that every role, no matter how small it seems, has its honor and is essential to the tapestry of life. His story reminds us that one need not be in the limelight to shine, nor in the annals of history to be remembered.

Unsung Pillars of the University of Scranton

3.105 Robert Nealis
Bookstore

In the echo of the corridors of the University of Scranton, past the shuffle of eager feet and the rustle of turned pages, there was a pulse to the campus life, a rhythm maintained by those whose names weren't etched into the stony facades of the institution but were inscribed in the more fleeting parchment of human memory. Robert Nealis was one such figure, a sentinel in the bookstore during the early 1970s, a period of tumult and transformation both within the university walls and beyond.

Nealis's domain was a treasure trove of knowledge, with stacks of textbooks that held the secrets of calculus and the charms of Chaucer. But more than a mere vendor of volumes, he was a steward of academia, facilitating the flow of information by ensuring that the right book found its way into anxious hands at the right time. His duties, though unheralded in the annals of academia, were pivotal. He sorted, he shelved, he sold. He was the custodian of queries, often guiding lost first-year students or the occasional perplexed professor to the correct aisle.

The challenges were as varied as the titles he tenderly cared for—late shipments, misprinted syllabi, and the perennial rush at the beginning of each semester. Yet, he met each with a steadfast resolve, a nod to the work ethic ingrained in the very air of Scranton, where the most significant generation toiled with quiet fortitude, not for acclaim but for the intrinsic reward of work well done.

Nealis might have seemed a mere cog in the academic machinery in that bustling bookstore. Still, to those who paused in their harried schedules to exchange a word or share a smile, he represented something more—a touchstone of dependability in the capricious currents of college life. His social standing was not marked by titles or accolades but by the respect accorded to one who sincerely serves.

Was his position fulfilling? One might surmise that he found purpose in the symphony of student dreams and aspirations. Though the tasks were repetitive, every book sold was a ticket to someone's future, every transaction a thread in the tapestry of educational endeavor.

Appreciation is a currency often scarce in the ledgers of the everyday worker, yet one hopes that Nealis felt the silent gratitude of those he served, the unspoken thanks of those he helped in small but significant ways.

And what of his legacy? It lies not in monuments of stone but in the fleeting moments of grace, the quiet satisfaction of duty performed with diligence, and the collective memory of generations who might not recall his name but who were the beneficiaries of his labor. In the end, Robert Nealis's legacy is the University of Scranton itself—the students he empowered, the institution he served, and the chapter he contributed to the ongoing story of a community's relentless pursuit of knowledge.

Unsung Pillars of the University of Scranton

3.106 Sandra Nitch
Education Department

In the corridors of the University of Scranton's Education Department, back when the early '70s were painting their vibrant strokes across the canvas of American history, you'd have found Sandra Nitch. An employee whose specific duties were not etched into the records for posterity but whose impact, like the countless others in her generation, was indelibly marked by a staunch work ethic that Scranton knew all too well.

Sandra, whose last name echoed a niche — a fitting metaphor for her specialized role — may have juggled many tasks. Picture her organizing curriculum materials, coordinating with faculty on the latest educational theories, or assisting in developing teacher preparation programs. Her days were likely a blend of the clerical and the cerebral, a mediator between the department's lofty academic goals and the grounded, day-to-day operations that kept the machine well-oiled.

The challenges she faced were probably as varied as the courses offered. There were new educational trends to keep abreast of, a society in flux to respond to, and the constant striving to ensure that the teachers they molded would be equipped for the real-world classrooms they'd soon lead. It was a time when education was seen as a transfer of knowledge and a critical tool for social change.

Unsung Pillars of the University of Scranton

While not headlined in faculty newsletters, Sandra's role in the department was the kind that held things together. Perhaps she worked closely with students, offering them counsel and administrative guidance, or maybe her tasks were more behind the scenes — organizing events, managing budgets, or liaising between departments. Whatever her day-to-day, it was undoubtedly vital, the kind of work that doesn't consistently get recognized in grand ceremonies but is celebrated in the quiet nods of faculty and the grateful smiles of students.

Her social standing on campus? It might not have been public acclaim, but among those who worked with her, there was likely a deep respect for her commitment and her ability to get things done. She probably moved through the halls with quiet confidence, known to some and unknown to others but always integral.

As for fulfillment, one might imagine that for Sandra, satisfaction came not from accolades but from seeing a program successfully launched or a student teacher thanking her for indispensable advice. Her fulfillment was perhaps in the seamless execution of a complex schedule or the smooth start of a new semester.

The Education Department's philosophy at the time was probably one of nurturing not just educators but educators who were thinkers, leaders, and agents of change. They prepared individuals to shape young minds when the country grappled with profound social and political changes. With Sandra as part of its engine, the department likely focused on instilling in its students an ethos of responsibility — to educate with purpose, passion, and a sense of duty to the community.

Unsung Pillars of the University of Scranton

Her legacy at the university? It's woven into the institution's fabric in the generations of teachers who passed through its doors, equipped with the knowledge and the spirit to make a difference. It's a legacy that doesn't stand alone but is interlinked with the stories of all those whose work forms the backbone of an institution.

Sandra Nitch, then, embodies the spirit of her time and place — Scranton in the '70s, a period of determination and transition. Though not documented in the annals of history, her story resonates with the collective memory of a generation known for its perseverance and unwavering commitment to the common good.

Unsung Pillars of the University of Scranton

3.106 Sharon Nolan
Treasurer's Office

In the bustling corridors of the University of Scranton, amidst the tumultuous ebb and flow of the early 1970s, a steadfast figure named Sharon Nolan worked in the Treasurer's Office. She was not the kind of person who made headlines or whose name was etched into the cornerstone of buildings; instead, Sharon was a pillar of quiet strength and diligence, her hands as steady as her resolve, working with the meticulousness that the numbers demanded.

Her days were woven with the fabric of financial records, the threads of debit and credit intertwining under her watchful eye. As a guardian of the university's purse strings, Sharon's responsibilities extended far beyond mere calculation. She was an unsung architect of the institution's future, ensuring that scholarships were funded, facilities were maintained, and the gears of academia turned smoothly.

Challenges were as frequent as they were varied – from the intricacies of financial regulations to the unpredictability of economic tides. Yet, Sharon faced them with an unwavering work ethic, a trait as ingrained in her as the coal seams running beneath the Scranton soil. While not glamorous, her position was a fulfilling marathon of service punctuated by the silent satisfaction of a ledger balanced to the last penny.

Unsung Pillars of the University of Scranton

Sharon's social standing on campus was much like that of Scranton's iron railings: frank, reliable, and often overlooked until needed. She was the heartbeat of the office, and her presence was felt in every budget meeting and financial report. Did she feel appreciated? Perhaps in the way true pillars of a community are – not always celebrated, but ever essential.

Sharon's legacy at the University of Scranton is not enshrined in a plaque or a portrait. Instead, it is in the quiet assurance that, for a time, the financial stewardship of the university was in capable hands. It is in the generation of students who graduated, perhaps oblivious to her role in their education, but whose lives were indelibly shaped by her dedication. It is in the integrity and commitment that she brought to her work every day, a testament to the enduring work ethic of Scranton.

Sharon Nolan was a name that would not echo through the halls of fame but would be whispered with respect in the hushed tones of those who understood the value of steadfast dedication to duty. Her story is a mosaic of everyday resilience, a life measured not in accolades but in the unwavering constancy of purpose.

Unsung Pillars of the University of Scranton

3.107 Caryl Notchick
Business Department

In the fabric of Scranton's academic tapestry during the early 1970s, threads of diligence and aspiration were woven deeply. At the University of Scranton, one such thread was Caryl Notchick, a name not emblazoned on plaques but etched in the memory of many. In the Department of Business and Economics, her role as faculty secretary was less about the title and more about being the unseen hand that kept the academic gears turning.

Caryl's day would begin with the clack of typewriter keys, letters forming the correspondence and documents crucial for the Department's functions. Her responsibilities stretched from scheduling meetings to managing faculty records, from assisting in curriculum development to aiding students lost in the bureaucratic maze. She was the connective tissue between faculty and the administration, between students and the knowledge they sought.

The Department itself was a bustling hub, its teachings a blend of theory and practicality, providing students with the tools to understand and navigate the shifting economic landscapes of the time. Though not directly educational, Caryl's role was pivotal in facilitating this knowledge transfer. She coordinated class schedules, prepared materials for lectures, and sometimes served

Unsung Pillars of the University of Scranton

as a confidante to students overwhelmed by the rigors of academia.

With its coal-mining heritage, Scranton was a community that valued hard work and perseverance. Caryl, a local Fell Township High School graduate, embodied these values. By day, she contributed to the university's mission. By night, she toiled towards her degree in sociology, her presence in classrooms after hours a testament to her belief in lifelong learning.

Her position, while fulfilling, was not without challenges. The academic environment of the 1970s was in flux, with societal changes reflected in the student body's attitudes and the faculty's perspectives. Balancing the old with the new ensuring the Department did not falter amidst these shifts, was a daily test of her adaptability and resolve.

On campus, Caryl's social standing was that of a bridge-builder. She was not the professor in the limelight, but her influence was felt by all who passed through the Department's doors. Appreciation for her was often shown in quiet acknowledgments. The knowing nods of faculty and the grateful smiles of students she had assisted.

When considering her legacy, it's not found in the annals of academic journals but in the successes of those she helped mold. For many, she was the University of Scranton's unsung hero, her work ethic reflecting the Scranton area's spirit. Her legacy is one of dedication, service, and an unwavering commitment to the betterment of both individuals and the institution she served. It's a legacy that whispers through the halls, a soft but persistent echo of a time when a secretary's typewriter was as vital as the professor's lecture.

Unsung Pillars of the University of Scranton

3.108 Anthony Noto
Residence Halls

In the early morning hours, when the mist still clung to the grounds of the University of Scranton, Anthony S. Noto was already hours into his day. As a maintenance supervisor, his hands told the stories of his work—each callus and scar a chapter of diligence. The residence halls stood sturdy and welcoming, a testament to Anthony's silent guardianship. His responsibilities were many, but his commitment to the job meant that each light bulb replaced and every leaky faucet fixed contributed to the well-being of the university community.

The challenges were as relentless as the seasons—harsh winters tested the infrastructure's resilience, and the students' youthful exuberance often resulted in wear and tear that demanded not just a maintenance supervisor's skill but also a parent's patience. Yet, Anthony found fulfillment in the very fabric of these challenges. The clang of his toolbox was a familiar symphony in the halls, and while his role was often behind the scenes, the smooth operation of the dorms spoke volumes of his contribution.

His social standing on campus was not measured in accolades but in the quiet nods of appreciation from the faculty, the thankful smiles of the students, and the camaraderie amongst his team. Though his position was not glamorous, the sense of community he fostered through his work was his reward. He was a figure known to many, a constant in an ever-changing academic landscape, and his presence was a reassurance of continuity and care.

After his years at the university, Anthony moved on to the Dunmore Lumber Company, where the skills he honed at the university aided him until his retirement. Home life was his sanctuary, where he was not just a supervisor but a husband and a father. His legacy was not etched in stone but in the lives of his family and the students whose college experiences were made better by his silent vigilance.

A devout man, he found solace and strength in his faith at Saint Francis of Assisi Church, and through his active participation in the South Scranton Residents Association, he extended his service to a broader community.

When Anthony passed in 1991, he left behind more than just a memory; he left a blueprint of service and a legacy of quiet dedication that shaped not just the physical but also the moral landscape of the University of Scranton. His final resting place in Cathedral Cemetery lies beneath the soil of the city he helped build, not just through brick and mortar but through the strength of his character and the warmth of his heart.

Unsung Pillars of the University of Scranton

3.109 Alex Obidinski
Groundsman

A steady presence in the quiet cloisters of the University of Scranton marked the early '70s: a man who bent his back under the weight of the seasons—Alex Obidinski, the groundsman. As the Pennsylvania sky stretched above, Alex wove his diligence into the campus fabric each day. He was the custodian of nature's flux, tending to the lush lawns, the burgeoning flowers in spring, and the relentless snowfall in winter.

His were the hands that shaped the university's face; it was a canvas upon which he painted with mower and shovel. The challenges were many—the temperamental whims of weather, the ceaseless cycle of growth and decay, and the ever-watchful eyes of academia. Yet, there was fulfillment in the symphony of his tasks, from the most straightforward wedding to the grand orchestration of preparing for commencement ceremonies.

His was a life of service, etched deeply by the trials of the Second World War in the Pacific, where courage earned him a Bronze Star. The discipline and camaraderie of military life never left him, manifesting in his dedication to his work, the Embury United Methodist Church, and the John J. Michaels VFW post.

Scranton's soil was his teacher, from the classrooms of its public schools to the wisdom he gathered at Scranton Technical High

Unsung Pillars of the University of Scranton

School. Before the university called, he shaped the land with a construction company and poured generosity at the Friendly Tavern, a testament to his belief in community and fellowship.

Alex's legacy at the university is not just in the grounds he maintained but in the quiet example he set. His stewardship over the green spaces provided a serene backdrop for thousands of students and staff who may not have known his name but felt the care he invested in their environment.

He left behind a family—his widow and three daughters—echoes of his love and commitment and a plot at Fairlawn Cemetery, where the grass whispers his contributions to the world. In the hallowed halls of the university, in the murmurs of the church, and the camaraderie at the VFW, his legacy endures—a steadfast guardian of growth, both of the land and of the spirit.

Unsung Pillars of the University of Scranton

3.110 Arlene Olivetti
Library

In the early 1970s, Arlene Olivetti was a fixture in the hushed corridors of the University of Scranton's library. Each day, she would assume her post with a sense of unwavering dedication, a guardian and guide amidst rows of books that were her charges as much as the students she assisted. Her role was multifaceted – cataloging new acquisitions, aiding in research, and often, simply listening to those who needed more than academic support.

The challenges were as varied as the library's collection. Technology was changing; the clang of the typewriter was slowly giving way to the hum of computers, and Arlene was at the forefront of this transition, adapting with a mixture of enthusiasm and caution. The card catalog, her familiar friend, now had to share space with electronic databases, a sign of times both exciting and daunting.

This era was a transition not just for technology but for society. Arlene's work in the library became a subtle act of service amidst the backdrop of social upheaval. She offered a stable refuge where debates could rage in books and periodicals rather than between the individuals who sought solace in the library's neutral space.

Unsung Pillars of the University of Scranton

For Arlene, fulfillment was found in the success of the students she aided, in the moments of discovery and understanding she helped foster. The gratitude of a student who had mastered a challenging topic or the appreciation of a colleague for her meticulous organization was the simple affirmation of her significant role.

Fellow staff saw her as a pillar – reliable and steadfast. Students, with the egotism of youth, might not have always shown their appreciation. Still, there was an unspoken respect for her knowledge and her willingness to aid in their academic journeys.

Arlene Olivetti's legacy at the University of Scranton is etched not just in the library's ledgers or the systems she helped implement but also in the minds and futures of those she touched. Her commitment to knowledge and service remains a quiet benchmark for those who followed, an example of how the heart of a university does not always beat in classrooms but sometimes in the modest company of books and the people who shepherd them.

Unsung Pillars of the University of Scranton

3.111 George Onofrey
Cafeteria

In the heart of Scranton, in the bustling corridors of the university, George Onofrey was a figure as constant as turning pages in the many books that surrounded him. His domain was the cafeteria, where the scent of coffee blended with the chatter of young minds. It was the early 1970s, and George, clad in a modest uniform, was the silent sentinel of sustenance.

His days were rhythmic, dictated by the pulse of student life. He was there before the dawn touched the windows, firing up the stoves, his hands moving with practiced certainty. He knew the cafeteria like a well-loved book, each appliance a familiar chapter, every recipe a memorized verse.

The challenges were as numerous as the students he fed. He juggled the logistics of supply orders with the unpredictability of youthful appetites, all while keeping a vigilant eye on the budget. The machinery was temperamental, prone to fits and starts, yet George's patience seemed infinite.

To the onlooker, it might have seemed a thankless task, yet fulfillment was woven into the fabric of his work. Fulfillment came in small servings: a smile from a homesick freshman, the raucous laughter of a table shared by friends, the quiet thanks

Unsung Pillars of the University of Scranton

from a professor working late. They were the secret ingredients in his daily routine, the spices that flavored his labor.

Appreciation is a currency often spent sparingly in the hustle of academia, but George found wealth in nods and brief exchanges. The staff, his comrades in arms, shared knowing glances as they orchestrated the ballet of the lunch rush. The students, often lost in their thoughts and deadlines, might not have known his name, but they recognized the steadiness of his presence.

Legacy is an elusive dish to prepare, particularly in the transient world of a university. Yet, George's legacy was as nourishing as the meals he so diligently prepared. Long after the echoes of his work faded, stories remained, tales shared over coffee about the man who helped turn a university cafeteria into a patchwork of memories. In this place, everyone, for a moment, could feel at home.

George Onofrey, in his quiet corner of the University of Scranton, was a weaver of community, his threads running unseen through the tapestry of countless lives. His was a legacy not of monuments but of moments, the simple, profound touchstones of daily life that, like his perfectly brewed coffee, were a warm, welcoming presence in the ebb and flow of university life.

3.112 Rose Orlando
Cafeteria

In the early 1970s, when the world was a tapestry of movements and change, a subtle yet touching tradition bloomed quietly within the heart of the University of Scranton. It was in this landscape of academia and youthful ambition that Rose Orlando found her calling. As an employee in the university's cafeteria, Rose was more than just a staff member; she was a fixture of the daily lives of countless students, a bearer of comfort in the form of sustenance and a warm smile.

The duties of a cafeteria worker in those days were manifold, far beyond the simple serving of meals. They required one to be part chef, cleaner, counselor, and sometimes confidante. The challenges were as accurate as they were varied – managing the surge of students with their diverse palates, dealing with the scarcity of supplies that the 70s' economy often imposed, and the physical demands of being on one's feet all day. Yet, in this very crucible, Rose shone the brightest, turning challenges into opportunities for kindness and connection.

Her fulfillment did not stem from accolades or grand gestures but from the daily gratitude of students who found a piece of home in her dishes, the camaraderie with her fellow staff who shared her dedication, and the personal satisfaction of a job well done. The students may not have always said it, but their smiles spoke volumes, and their occasional thanks were treasures she held dear.

It was in 1970 that Rose's inherent warmth became a public emblem of the university's spirit. As first-year students arrived, nervous and eager, with mothers in tow, clutching at the apron strings of home, Rose was there. With a simple gesture – the gifting of a long-stemmed rose – she did more than welcome them; she reassured them. It was a symbol, a promise that they would be educated and cared for here, at the University of Scranton.

Rose's legacy is not etched in stone monuments or captured in grand portraits that line the hallowed halls of academia. Instead, it is woven into the memories of those who passed through the university during her time. Her legacy is a reminder that the heart of an institution is not its curriculum or facilities but the people who breathe life into it every day. For many, Rose Orlando was the University of Scranton – a figure synonymous with a time when the world was changing, and yet some things – like kindness, care, and a welcoming smile – remained steadfastly the same.

3.112 Benny Pambianco
Cafeteria

Benny Pambianco stood behind the steaming counter with the assuredness of someone who had found his calling among pots and spoons. In the bustling cafeteria of the University of Scranton, he was a conductor orchestrating a symphony of flavors for the palate of academia. It was the early 70s, a time of change and challenge, but in Benny's kitchen, the only revolutions were culinary.

His day would start before the sun peeked over the horizon of Eynon, his hometown. By the time the first rays of light cut through the morning mist, Benny would be in the kitchen, his hands already busy prepping for the day. His duties were manifold, from crafting menus to ensuring each dish that left his kitchen met his exacting standards. He juggled the logistics of supply with the creativity of cooking, often innovating with limited resources.

The challenges were many. The palates of students and faculty were evolving, demanding more than the standard fare. Benny rose to the occasion, infusing his dishes with traditional flavors and contemporary twists. Yet, the actual test was not in food preparation but in the garnishing of relationships. Benny knew each student by name, and his kitchen became a haven where homesick young adults found comfort in his hearty stews and wisecracks.

In the kitchen's heat, Benny found fulfillment. Each thank-you, each contented sigh after a meal, was a note in the melody of his satisfaction. He was appreciated, not just by fellow staff but by those who mattered most—the students. They saw in him not just a chef but a mentor, a friend, a confidante.

His legacy? It was not just in the recipes he left behind, but in the lives he touched. Benny Pambianco was remembered for his warmth to the cafeteria and how he turned a simple meal into a convivial feast. It was said you could taste the love in his food—a passion that extended beyond the kitchen to his beloved Bernice, his partner in life for 64 years, to his children, whom he raised with the same devotion he applied to his culinary creations.

Benny's life was seasoned with the things he cherished most—family, patriotism, and the simple joys of walking his dog, Rascal. Even as a proud Steelers fan, his heart was always with his family and community. When he hung up his apron, the university lost more than a chef; it lost a piece of its heart.

As Benny passed on to the grand kitchen beyond, those he left behind remembered him not with sorrow but with a smile, the kind of knowing someone lived well, loved much, and cooked with all his heart. Benny Pambianco, a chef in a small university town, left behind flavors that lingered long after the last dish was cleared, flavors of a prosperous life.

Unsung Pillars of the University of Scranton

3.113 Chiara Persichetti
Library

Chiara Persichetti's story is woven through the quiet halls of the University of Scranton's library, where the rustle of pages and the faint scent of aging paper were ever-present. In the early 1970s, when computers were not yet the heart of the library, Chiara was the human nexus of knowledge, a guardian of the printed word.

Her days were filled with the meticulous cataloging of new acquisitions, the precise shelving of returned literature, and the gentle guiding of students through the maze of the Dewey Decimal System. She was a detective, helping to unearth obscure references for term papers and thesis projects, her eyes always reflecting a gleam of satisfaction when a student's face lit up with discovering the perfect source.

Challenges were as constant as the steady tick of the library clock. Chiara faced the daunting task of keeping the ever-growing collection organized and accessible while adapting to the evolving landscape of information retrieval, which was just beginning to feel the ripples of the digital revolution.

In this sanctum of study, she found fulfillment. There was a harmony in the order of books, a rhythm to the academic year, and a melody in the interactions with curious minds. Though

Unsung Pillars of the University of Scranton

quiet and unassuming, Chiara's presence was a steady force; her knowledge and helpfulness were foundations upon which many students built their academic success.

Appreciation for Chiara's work was a soft murmur, like the hushed tones used between the stacks. Her sister, a faculty member at a local college, often heard accolades of her dedication in the academic circles they shared. While her other brother, a senior officer in the Italian army, stood a world apart, Chiara's impact was no less strategic or vital in the lives of those she served.

Her legacy at the university is a tapestry of countless scholarly pursuits she supported, the grateful nods of students and faculty, and the silent rows of books that stood as sentinels to a career spent in the service of education.

Although Chiara's story ended in 1983 under the warm Italian sun, it remains etched in the University of Scranton's annals, a testament to the quiet yet indispensable role of those who serve the life of the mind.

Unsung Pillars of the University of Scranton

3.114 Dolores Pisarski
Admissions Office

In the fabric of the University of Scranton, woven through its corridors and classrooms, was a strong and steady thread: Dolores A. Pisarski. She wasn't just the senior administrator of the Admissions Office; she was the gatekeeper, the custodian of futures. In the early 1970s, a medium-sized university like Scranton was a microcosm of the world outside, a place simmering with the dreams of youth and the wisdom of academia.

Dolores' days were a tapestry of tasks, from evaluating applications to orchestrating open houses. She was the bridge between the student's aspirations and the university's standards, a meticulous manager ensuring that the incoming classes were not just numbers but a mosaic of potential.

The challenges were as varied as the applicants' essays. The 70s brought change, a shifting landscape of educational standards, and a need for inclusivity and diversity. Dolores navigated these waters gracefully, often the unseen hand guiding the university through the tumultuous tide of change.

Was the position fulfilling? For Dolores, it was more than a job; it was a calling. Each accepted application was a seed planted, each graduation a bloom she had a hand in nurturing. Her colleagues saw her dedication, her tireless work that often went beyond the call of duty, and in the quiet acknowledgment of peers, there was appreciation.

The students may not have known her by name, but they felt her presence and her commitment to their future. In 1982, the university recognized what many already knew, awarding her the Pro Deo et Universitate—For God and the University—an honor emblematic of her years of silent, steadfast service.

Beyond the hallowed halls, Dolores had another passion: golf. On the greens, just as in her office, she was known for her focus and finesse, a well-known figure in the local golfing community, her swing as sure as her decision-making.

To speak of Dolores A. Pisarski is to talk of a legacy—not just in the ledger of admissions but in the lives that passed through her office, forever altered by her commitment to education, the university, and the greater good.

Unsung Pillars of the University of Scranton

3.115 Marianne Pirino
Student Personnel Office

Marianne Pirino sat at her desk surrounded by the click-clack of typewriters and the intermittent bell ding signaling the end of a line. Her hands moved deftly over the keys, a ballet of administrative efficiency. She was a cornerstone of the Student Personnel Office at the University of Scranton in the early 1970s, an era marked by the earthy smell of mimeograph ink and the rustle of carbon copy paper.

Every day, Marianne was the unseen hand guiding students through their academic journeys. Her role was pivotal: she scheduled appointments, maintained student records, and answered a never-ending stream of inquiries with an almost saintly patience. The responsibilities of an administrative assistant in a bustling university office were manifold and often went unnoticed by those who didn't understand the intricacies of academia.

The challenges were as silent as they were significant. Marianne worked in a time when gender roles were rigidly defined, and the university setting was a bastion of male dominance, especially within the Catholic tradition that framed the institution's ethos. Yet, she navigated these waters with grace, her dedication unwavering, even if it went unrecognized by some.

Unsung Pillars of the University of Scranton

The fulfillment in her work didn't come from accolades but from the quiet satisfaction of a job well done and the success of the students she helped shepherd. She was a fixture, as constant as the university's brick-and-mortar. Marianne was indispensable to the students and staff who took the time to know her. Her knowledge of the university's policies was comprehensive, and her ability to ease student bureaucratic burdens was deeply appreciated.

In a world where her gender could have been a barrier, Marianne stood as a testament to quiet resilience. Her feelings about working in such an environment were complex: a tapestry of pride in her work and a silent yearning for a day when her contributions would be seen as equal to those of her male counterparts.

The University of Scranton during the early 1970s was a place of academic pursuit shadowed by the societal norms of the day. But within the walls of the Student Personnel Office, Marianne Pirino was a beacon of support, her legacy not in the name of a building but in the lives of students who might never know just how much she did to help them on their way.

3.116 Julia Pollack
Residence Halls

Julia M. Pollack's hands were rarely clean during the day. The smell of disinfectant and floor wax clung to her like a second skin, a testament to her dedication to the University of Scranton's residence halls. To the students bustling through the corridors, she was a fixture as reliable as the bricks and mortar themselves. Yet, in the grand tapestry of university life, she was often just a blur in the background, her story woven quietly into the larger narrative.

Julia's day began as the campus stirred to life, her cart laden with tools and cleaning supplies, her mission to ensure that each student could start their day in a clean and comfortable environment. The residence halls were her domain, and she tended to them with a meticulousness that spoke of pride. It was the 1970s, and the world was changing, but time seemed to follow its course within the university's walls.

The early mornings were hers alone, a solitary figure against the sprawling canvas of empty hallways. It was a meditative time when she could move unhurriedly, preparing the stage for the day's drama. Her responsibilities were many—cleaning, maintenance, and even minor repairs. The work was physical,

Unsung Pillars of the University of Scranton

the hours long, and the recognition scarce. Yet, Julia found fulfillment in the order she brought to the chaos of college life.

Challenges were part of the routine. Machinery broke down, budgets were tight, and the demands seemed endless. But there was also camaraderie among the staff. A shared sense of purpose bonded them. Management, often aloof, may not have always noted her efforts, but her colleagues did, and sometimes, so did the students, whose careless youth she tidied after without complaint.

In Scranton, a city that mirrored her steadfast character, Julia's role at the Catholic university was a quiet affirmation of the changing times—a woman carving a space for herself in a male-dominated institution. Her faith, a cornerstone of her life, found expression in her involvement with Saint Lucy's church. The community anchored her, where she served with the same humble dedication she gave to her work.

Her legacy was not in grand gestures or headlines but in the small acts of kindness, in floors polished to a shine, and in the quiet nod of acknowledgment in the hallway. It was a legacy of persistence and quiet dignity.

When the university president recognized Julia's service with the Order of Pro Deo Et Universitate, it was a rare moment in the spotlight—a nod to her years of unassuming service. But the applause of that day could not capture the daily victories. The lives touched in passing, the sense of place and home she helped to maintain for those far from their own.

Educated in Scranton's schools, living most of her life within its embrace, Julia's story was entwined with the city's own. When she passed, she left behind siblings, a community, and a university shaped by her hands in countless small ways.

Julia M. Pollack rests now in the Cathedral Cemetery beneath the same sky she lived under, in the city she helped, in her way, to build. Her story, like so many might have been overlooked, but for those who knew, who noticed, it was a tale of quiet strength, a narrative of steadfast service and devotion, both secular and sacred.

Unsung Pillars of the University of Scranton

3.117 Alfonso Raniella Estate

In the heart of Scranton, amongst the bustle of university life, there walked a man whose hands had been toughened by both the tools of construction and the weapons of war. Alfonso Raniella, a name known to the stones and timbers of the Jesuit residence known as the Estate, carried the quiet dignity of a life rich with varied experiences.

Alfonso's days were spent in the company of brick and mortar, his duties as vital to the Estate as the foundations it stood on. He was the one who patched the walls, who ensured the plumbing ran clear, and who could be found atop a ladder, making sure that even the highest windows let in the clear light of Pennsylvania skies. In a medium-sized university like Scranton, the staff maintaining the facilities were the unsung heroes, ensuring the seamless operation of an institution dedicated to higher learning.

The 1970s brought their own set of challenges. The tools were often essential, the work physically demanding, and the appreciation sporadic at best. Yet, Alfonso found fulfillment in this labor beyond the daily grind. Each fixed leak, each repaired stairwell, and each freshly painted wall was a testament to his dedication, a silent contribution to the education of hundreds.

Unsung Pillars of the University of Scranton

Management may have acknowledged his efforts with a nod or a word. Still, among his fellow staff, his work truly resonated with his reliability, which was a constant in an ever-changing campus life. Often caught up in their academic and social whirlwinds, students might overlook the man behind the maintenance, yet his impact was imprinted on their daily lives in myriad invisible ways.

In Scranton, Alfonso's status was that of a veteran, a craftsman, a blue-collar worker who carried with him the stories of the past and the skills of his trade. The university, a bastion of Catholic education and a male-dominated hierarchy might have seemed an unlikely place for a man of his background. Yet, he navigated it with the ease of someone who understands that institutions are made up of individuals and that every role, no matter how seemingly small, is crucial to the whole.

Reflecting on his time at the university, his feelings were complex—a blend of pride in his work and a veteran's understanding of deeper battles. The Estate was not just a residence but a symbol of the values he stood for: resilience, service, and a commitment to community.

Alfonso's legacy is not etched in the annals of academia but in the physical legacy of the spaces he maintained and the memories of those who knew the worth of his work. He was a resident, a builder by trade, a soldier by a call of duty, and a maintainer by choice, whose story interweaves with the fabric of Scranton itself, a narrative of quiet strength and enduring commitment.

Unsung Pillars of the University of Scranton

3.118 Anthony Redensky
Cafeteria

Anthony Redensky's story is interlaced with the aroma of freshly brewed coffee and the clatter of cutlery from the University of Scranton's cafeteria. As a member of the "Greatest Generation," he brought to his post-WWII life the same resilience and dedication that had seen him through the trials of global conflict. In the heart of the 1970s, amidst a world of change, his steadfast presence in the cafeteria was a constant for the university community.

The cafeteria, often bustling from dawn until dusk, was Anthony's realm. Here, he was part of a team that operated like a well-oiled machine, serving meals as much a part of the university experience as the lectures and libraries. He was there in the early hours, helping to prep for the breakfast rush, and often stayed late, ensuring that everything was set for the next day. The responsibility was significant, feeding hundreds of minds and shaping the future.

The challenges were many: managing the relentless pace of meal service, adhering to tight budgets, and meeting the varied dietary needs of a diverse student body. Yet, Anthony found in these challenges the same call to service that had defined his years in uniform. It was a different battlefield, but the mission was similar—to support and sustain.

Unsung Pillars of the University of Scranton

The appreciation for his work might not have always been overt. Still, it was there in the nods of students as they passed through his line, the camaraderie among the kitchen staff, and the occasional commendations from management. His was a service that underpinned the daily life of the university, a role that was as much about nurturing the community as it was about nourishing bodies.

In Scranton, a city of humble roots and hardworking people, Anthony reflected his generation's values: work ethic, community, and quiet patriotism. The university, with its Catholic roots and male-dominated hierarchy, was a microcosm of the world he had helped to shape—a world where his generation's contributions were foundational, even as the tides of change rolled in.

Working at the university offered Anthony a sense of continuation from his military service—a commitment to a cause greater than himself. It was a fulfillment not found in accolades but in the daily ritual of service, in the assurance that his role was vital to the fabric of university life.

His legacy is one of reliability, of the enduring spirit of a generation that had seen the worst and aimed for the best. Survived by a son and three sisters, Anthony's story didn't end with his passing. It lived on in the memories of those he served, the laughter and conversations that filled the cafeteria, and the legacy of service he passed down to his family.

Anthony Redensky now rests in Saint Stanislaus Cemetery, his stone among those of his peers—a generation marked by their service. In Scranton, and especially within the university, his legacy is carried forward by those who continue to serve, who see in their work not just a job but a calling.

Unsung Pillars of the University of Scranton

3.119 Joseph Reilly
Loyola Hall

In the early 1970s, a man named Joseph Reilly was beneath the newly risen edifice of Loyola Hall, with its pioneering green-tinted windows and Italian marble-infused tiles. Though unseen by the many who passed through the halls, his hands were part of the ligament and muscle that kept the heart of this university structure beating.

Joe was part of a team – a band of unsung heroes who wielded wrenches and pliers like artists with their brushes and chisels. Their canvas was the vast network of pipes, the labyrinth of wiring, and the gleaming floors that spoke of their unseen presence. They were the custodians of comfort, the wardens of warmth in winter, and the sentinels of calm during the dog days of summer.

His daily duties ranged from the mundane tightening of a loose screw to the critical monitoring of the heating systems that ensured the lecture halls remained sanctuaries of thought rather than chambers of chill. Joe and his team were troubleshooters in the most literal sense; each day presented a new puzzle, a challenge to be deciphered, a problem to be solved.

Unsung Pillars of the University of Scranton

The job was not without its challenges. The expectations were high, and the gratitude was often low. The building was a complex organism; like any living thing, it was unpredictable. Breakdowns and malfunctions were his dragons to slay, often at the most inopportune times. Yet, Joe found fulfillment in this. There was a silent pride in being the one who could and would fix anything.

Was his work appreciated? By some, certainly. The management knew the value of a well-oiled machine, and Joe's hands helped oil it. Fellow staff would nod in appreciation, knowing the comfort of their workspaces was his doing. And while students may not have known Joe by name, the smooth operation of their environment was a silent testament to his dedication.

In Scranton, a town of coal and steam, Joe's status was one of the everyman. He was one of many who worked behind the scenes, a part of the city's uncelebrated backbone. But Joe's role took on a deeper resonance within the walls of the University of Scranton, a Catholic institution. His work was a service, not just to a building or a school, but to a community of faith and learning.

And what of his legacy? Joe's legacy was not inscribed in the stone of Loyola Hall, but it stood firm, functional, and welcoming on countless days. It was in the smooth operation of Lynett Lecture Hall, the clarity of the sound from WUSV's steel tower, and the warmth of classrooms during winter lectures. Joe's legacy was the quiet assurance that there was a solution for every problem within these walls, a steady hand ready to restore balance. It was a legacy of reliability, service, and quiet pride in the unfailing function of a place dedicated to higher learning and higher purpose.

Unsung Pillars of the University of Scranton

3.120 Mary Ann Rempe
Research Bureau

Mary Ann Rempe's story is one of the threads in the intricate tapestry of the University of Scranton's history. As the backbone of the Research Bureau in the 1970s, a decade of change and challenge, she was the custodian of curiosity and a guardian of growth at a mid-sized Catholic university.

The Bureau, under her watch, was a hive of activity, a center where numbers and narratives converged. Here, research was not just academic; it was a bridge connecting the university to the broader world of Scranton and beyond. Mary Ann's role involved more than the meticulous gathering of data; it was about understanding the pulse of societal changes and how the institution could navigate and contribute to those changes.

Her daily duties were as diverse as they were demanding. She was an organizer, a facilitator, and sometimes, a mediator between the ambitious goals of academia and the stark realities of practical application. She administered surveys, compiled findings, and presented data that would often inform significant decisions of the university's path forward.

The challenges? They were as present as the opportunities. Balancing the rigors of academic integrity with the practicalities of resource limitations was a tightrope walk. Deadlines loomed, expectations soared, and Mary Ann's resolve never wavered.

Though shadowed by the enormity of its responsibility, this position brought fulfillment in unexpected ways. Each successful study influenced each policy, and each student's perspective broadened a notch in the measure of their accomplishment.

Appreciation is often a silent companion to such roles, but in her case, it came through. The management understood the weight of her contributions. Fellow staff leaned on her reliability. And the students, perhaps unknowingly, reaped the fruits of her labor in the enhanced quality of their education.

In Scranton, Mary Ann's status was emblematic of a generation of women forging paths in domains that were just beginning to open to them. Her role at the university mirrored the city's ethos - hard work, dedication, and a touch of pioneering spirit.

Working at the University of Scranton, particularly within its Catholic tradition, in the early 1970s offered a unique vantage point. It was a time of questioning and exploring how faith and reason, tradition, and innovation could coexist and enrich each other. Mary Ann's work, her very presence, became a testament to this exploration, to the blending of old and new, of faith and facts.

Her legacy? It's etched in the generations of students whose educational experiences were shaped by the data and decisions she helped to mold. It's in the progress the university made, guided by the light of her research. And it's in the quiet advancement of women's roles in academia and administration, a path she helped pave simply by showing up, day after day, committed to her role in the significant undertaking of education.

Unsung Pillars of the University of Scranton

Unsung Pillars of the University of Scranton

3.121 Michael Rencavage
Residence Halls

In the early 1970s, tucked away in the quiet town of Scranton, a man named Michael busied himself in the hallways and dorm rooms of a mid-sized Catholic university. His hands, often stained with the day's work, were a testament to the unending tasks that awaited him each morning. As a maintenance man, he was the ligament that connected the institution's life, a silent guardian of order and functionality.

Michael's days began with the sunrise, his tools clanging softly in the crisp morning air. He carried a hefty ring of keys that jingled with each step, a symphony of access to every nook and cranny within the university's embrace. His responsibilities were as varied as his problems: fixing leaky faucets, ensuring the heat ran smoothly through the veins of the old buildings, and replacing bulbs so that learning could flourish under the glow of his efforts.

The challenges were as relentless as the seasons. Winters were fierce, with pipes threatening to freeze and the old heaters groaning under the weight of expectation. Summers brought a different kind of trial, with the hum of fans battling the heat that clung stubbornly to the classrooms. Yet, through it all, Michael's resolve never wavered.

Unsung Pillars of the University of Scranton

This position, while often overlooked, was profoundly fulfilling for him. The quiet nods of thanks from passing staff and the shy smiles of students who watched him work his magic on a stubborn window were the moments that wove a tapestry of quiet satisfaction. Management knew his worth, his name synonymous with reliability, and his fellow staff saw him as the backbone of the day-to-day life at the university.

In Scranton, a town that valued hard work and modesty, Michael's status was that of a silent hero. He was one of many who kept the wheels turning, who ensured that life could go on unimpeded by the trivial inconveniences of a broken door or a flickering light.

Working at a Catholic institution in those times was to be part of a more prominent family, a community bound by shared beliefs and a collective purpose. Michael saw his work as an extension of these values, each stroke of his hammer contributing to the greater good, each twist of his wrench a tightening of the communal bond.

As for his legacy, it is not found in grand gestures or named buildings. Instead, it lives in the smooth hinges of doors that don't squeak, in the warmth of rooms during winter's assault, and in the grateful glances of those he helped, often without their knowing. Michael Rencavage, whose name was but a whisper on a roster, left a legacy of steadfast dedication, a quiet reminder of the dignity of labor and the uncelebrated heroism of maintenance in the heartbeat of an educational institution.

Unsung Pillars of the University of Scranton

3.122 Helen Riddilla
Estate

Helen Riddilla's story begins in the heart of Scranton, where the church spires outnumber the high-rises, and everyone's grandmother makes a better pasta sauce than the last. It was the sort of community where roots ran deep, and Helen's was no exception. Her parents were hardworking folks, symbolic of the town's spirit, and from them, she inherited a resilience that would come to define her career.

When Helen found her way to the University of Scranton in the early 1970s, it was as if she had entered a world apart, both challenging and comforting in its familiarity. As a maintenance staff member, her days were a tapestry of routine and unexpected turns. Her title was simple, "domestic," but it belied the complexity of her role. She was part custodian, part guardian of the Jesuit Home known as the estate. Her duties stretched from the crack of dawn's harsh light to the soft glow of dusk, encompassing everything from polishing the age-old woodwork to ensuring that the heating systems hummed reliably through the biting Scranton winters.

The environment she worked in was as solemn and grand as the Catholic traditions it upheld. Every corridor echoed with the steps of scholars and the whispers of prayer, and every room was a silent witness to the history it housed. Helen's role within this sacred space was unobtrusive yet foundational. She crept, ensuring the estate's dignity was preserved through meticulous care.

But the job was not without its challenges. The era's technology was basic, requiring an often-undervalued brand of physical labor. Budgets were tight, and the appreciation for such indispensable work was often expressed more in nods and smiles than in tangible rewards. Yet, Helen took pride in her work, finding fulfillment not in accolades but in the knowledge that her efforts contributed to the greater good of the university's mission.

Her relationships within the university were a mosaic of brief encounters and deep, unspoken understandings. Helen's interactions with her co-workers, the management, and the students were marked by mutual respect and the occasional friction that is inevitable in any close-knit community. Still, there was a camaraderie there. A shared sense of purpose bound them.

Helen might have admitted to a sense of pride in her work in her more reflective moments. There was a fulfillment in knowing that the cleanliness and order she brought to the estate were her contributions to the institution's legacy. She was part of something larger than herself, a thread in the tapestry of the university's storied history.

Her impact was felt in the smooth running of the estate, in the untroubled days of the residents and staff who might never know her name but would always feel the effects of her labor. She was appreciated quietly: a nod here, a thank you there, and the rare but cherished acknowledgment at staff meetings.

In the broader community of Scranton, Helen was one of many who upheld the town's values through her dedication to work and community. Like her character, her job was respected, reflecting the town's work ethic and its value of service.

Helen's legacy at the University of Scranton is not enshrined in plaques or statues but in the continued reverence for the spaces she maintained. She is remembered in the memories of those who worked alongside her, in the stories passed down through generations of university staff, and in the enduring quality of the estate itself.

The 1970s were a time of change, but for Helen, the era was defined by constancy and devotion. The era's social currents shaped her experiences, yet her story is timeless—a testament to the unseen individuals who are the heartbeat of any institution.

Looking back from today's vantage point, Helen's story is a window into a time when the Catholic identity of an institution like the University of Scranton was a cornerstone of its existence. Working there then was to be a part of a continuum that has evolved with technology and shifting social norms but remains rooted in the tradition of service. Helen Riddilla, a humble staff member, emerges as an unsung hero, her narrative a poignant piece of the university's rich mosaic.

3.123 Mary Ann Riebe
Computer Center

In the early 1970s, nestled within the heart of Scranton, there was a pulse, a hum of modern machinery that signaled a new era—the University Computer Center at the University of Scranton. Mary Ann Riebe lent her skills and spirit to this mid-sized Catholic college.

Mary Ann, a native to the coal-streaked landscapes of Pennsylvania, held a quiet demeanor shaped by a family of hard workers and a keen mind honed by an education that straddled the classics and the burgeoning field of computing. Drawn to the University of Scranton through proximity and the promise of being part of something cutting-edge, she found her place amid reels of tape and the clatter of punch cards.

As an employee in the Computer Center, Mary Ann's days were filled with the careful choreography of maintaining the mainframe, the behemoth at the heart of the center. She was responsible for ensuring that students and faculty could rely on this digital titan for their academic endeavors. The staff, a blend of academic wanderers and sharp-minded locals, were a testament to the times—more driven by passion and curiosity than formal qualifications.

Unsung Pillars of the University of Scranton

The challenges were as tangible as the hardware they grappled with—limited technology, budgets stretched thin, and the constant need to educate and re-educate a community inching into the digital age. Yet, these were the forge for triumphs, small victories that, when stitched together, formed the tapestry of progress.

Among her peers, Mary Ann's presence was steady, her contributions often acknowledged in the subtle nods of faculty and the grateful smiles of students whose theses were saved from the brink by her timely interventions. Her relationship with management was mutual respect, a shared understanding that they were all custodians of a future they were still mapping.

In Scranton, she held a status that was a blend of respect and curiosity—a woman in a field just beginning to open its doors wider to her gender, a pioneer in an institution where tradition and innovation were in constant dialogue.

Working within the framework of a Catholic institution brought its color to Mary Ann's reflections. There was a sense of community, shared values, and a mission that extended beyond the confines of the campus. It was a backdrop that underscored the importance of service and the pursuit of knowledge for her.

Her legacy, while not etched in the grand annals of history, remains in the memories of those who worked alongside her, the students who went on to shape the world with the knowledge she helped them access, and in the ethos of the Computer Center, which continues to evolve in the spirit of its early architects.

The 1970s wrapped Mary Ann's world in a tapestry of social change, economic upheavals, and political shifts, each thread influencing the fabric of her everyday life. Her narrative is a

Unsung Pillars of the University of Scranton

reminder of how the past, with its challenges and norms, informs the present. It provides a lens through which to view the role of religion, education, and technology in society's continuous march forward.

Mary Ann Riebe's story, a single thread in the larger narrative of the University of Scranton, speaks to the quiet revolution that personal dedication can bring about, an ode to those who work behind the scenes, their names known but a few, their impact resonating far beyond their imagining.

Unsung Pillars of the University of Scranton

3.124 Mirtha Rospigliosi
Financial Aid Office

Mirtha Rospigliosi's journey from the vibrant coast of Callao in Lima to the historic halls of the University of Scranton is a tale of ambition fueled by a dedication to service. A graduate of Callao High School and the Peruvian Institute of Business Administration, Mirtha carried the warmth of Peru to the colder climes of Pennsylvania. As a senior administrator in the financial aid office in the early 1970s, she found herself in the pulsating heart of the university's mission to make education accessible.

The financial aid office was a bustling hub staffed with individuals whose qualifications spanned the spectrum of experience in educational administration and accounting. Mirtha's unique background brought an international perspective to a team navigating the complexities of grants, scholarships, and student loans. Their duties were manifold, from meticulous record-keeping to the sensitive task of advising families on their financial options.

Challenges were inherent in the role. Technological tools were rudimentary by today's standards, and the personal touch was not just preferred but necessary. The office's typewriters clacked with the sounds of progress, and the filing cabinets held stories of hopes and dreams. This was an era when a computer was a luxury, not a given, and each application was a paper gateway to potential.

Unsung Pillars of the University of Scranton

For Mirtha, the fulfillment of her role was evident in the faces of the students she aided. Her efforts, a blend of administrative prowess and heartfelt empathy did not go unnoticed. Recognized by her peers, management, and the students whose lives she touched, Mirtha received a service award that acknowledged her commitment beyond the call of duty.

In Scranton, a city where community ties run deep, Mirtha held a special status. The local people saw her as an administrator and a beacon of diversity and strength within the Catholic institution's framework. Her dedication to the university's mission resonated with the city's values of hard work and community service.

Working within the Catholic ethos of the University of Scranton, Mirtha navigated her role gracefully, understanding the delicate balance between the university's religious identity and the secular needs of its students. The Catholic identity of the institution was a silent partner in every decision made, an ethos of care and community that aligned with her values.

Mirtha's legacy is etched in the ledger of the university's history and in the lives of the students she empowered. Under her tenure, the University of Scranton's financial aid office of the early 1970s became a place where financial barriers were dismantled, one student at a time.

Reflecting on the era, the contrast with today's world is stark. Technology has transformed the financial aid landscape, yet the essence of the role — to facilitate education — remains unchanged. Mirtha's story is a reminder of the timeless nature of service and the enduring value of an education advocate who crossed continents to make a difference. Her narrative is a

Unsung Pillars of the University of Scranton

testament to the power of personal touch in an increasingly impersonal world and a celebration of the human spirit's capacity to connect, support, and uplift.

3.125 Mary Ryan
Counseling Center

In the heart of Scranton, amidst the change that the 1970s brought, there worked a secretary in the Guidance department of the University of Scranton, known to all as Mary Noone Ryan. A local through and through, Mary's roots ran as deep as the coal mines, her life story woven into the city's fabric.

Her journey was marked by personal loss; the widow of John Ryan, her resilience shone through the quiet halls of Holy Rosary Church, where she sought solace and purpose. Her academic prowess was evident. A graduate of Saint Cecilia's Academy and the esteemed Wharton School of Finance at the University of Pennsylvania, a testament to her intellect and ambition.

Before her quarter-century tenure at the university, Mary's skills honed the narratives at the Scranton Times, where she worked as secretary to the founder. This experience would prove invaluable as she transitioned to the university's Guidance Department, a place of hope and future-making for young minds.

Unsung Pillars of the University of Scranton

The department was staffed with counselors, administrative assistants, and support staff, each a specialist in nurturing student potential. The qualifications ranged from degrees in psychology to education. All united in the mission to guide. Mary's role was pivotal, her days a symphony of schedules, confidential files, and the gentle art of listening. Her responsibilities were the lifeblood of the department, ensuring the seamless operation of guidance activities.

The era's challenges were the clunky typewriters, the absence of digital databases, and the weight of paper that told stories of aspirations. But Mary, with her indomitable spirit, thrived. Her position was not just fulfilling; it was her calling, her efforts a beacon of dedication that management, staff, and students deeply appreciated.

In Scranton, Mary's status transcended her job. She was a pillar, her very name synonymous with steadfastness and grace. Her work at the Catholic institution was more than a job; it was a continuation of her faith, her service a form of prayer.

Her feelings about the university reflected a complex blend of pride and humility. She was proud to serve, to be a part of shaping futures, yet humbled by the magnitude of her role. The Pro Deo et Universitate award for 25 years of service was not just a recognition of time but an acknowledgment of her heart's work.

Mary's legacy lies in the lives she touched, the guidance she offered, and the strength she embodied. Her quiet yet firm support echoed in the university's corridors long after retirement. She was remembered for her contributions to the institution and her role in the community, where she served with the same enthusiasm outside the university, connected to the city's Catholic and social fabric.

Unsung Pillars of the University of Scranton

The 1970s were a time of transformation, and Mary Noone Ryan stood as a testament to the enduring values amidst that change. Her story, a chapter in the university's history, highlights one individual's impact on an institution and a community. It invites reflection on the role of Catholic education in changing times. It serves as a bridge between the personal touch of the past and the technological advances of the future. Mary Noone Ryan is a name etched in the annals of the University of Scranton, a legacy of service and dedication.

3.126 Ceil Rybitski
Cafeteria

Ceil F. Rybitski, a steadfast presence in the University of Scranton's cafeteria, was a figure as constant in the lives of many as the daily breaking of bread. Her story is one steeped in the resilience and nurturing spirit that characterized the city of Scranton itself.

Ceil's journey began and ended in Scranton, her life's bookends mirroring the city's narrative of hard work and community. Widowed early, with the passing of her husband in 1951, she wove her life with threads of tenacity, working not only for the university but also for a silk mill, showcasing the dynamic spirit of the time.

The cafeteria she served was a microcosm of the university, staffed by a diligent crew whose qualifications were as much about their ability to serve with kindness as their culinary skills. Ceil's role, though not officially recorded, was undeniably vital. She was the unseen hand, ensuring the students and staff were nourished in body and spirit.

Unsung Pillars of the University of Scranton

Ceil's daily routine was one of early starts, steaming pots, and the clatter of dishes. Each task, from peeling potatoes to ladling soup, was performed with a mother's care. The challenges were many: managing the rush of hungry students, ensuring the quality of meals with limited resources, and the physical toll such work takes. Yet she stood undaunted, a testament to her enduring strength.

Her position was more than fulfilling; it was a mission. Ceil's efforts were the silent foundation upon which the academic life rested. She was appreciated by all – management, staff, and students alike – her presence a comforting constant in the swiftly changing tides of college life.

In Scranton, Ceil's status was akin to an unsung hero. Her dedication to her work at the university, a prestigious Catholic institution, was mirrored in her devout life, serving as president of the Christian Mothers at Sacred Hearts of Jesus and Mary church. Her faith and work were intertwined, each feeding into the other, providing sustenance and sanctuary to those she served.

Ceil's legacy in the university's history is indelible. She nourished thousands, her kindness and resilience a lesson in themselves. Her memory is preserved in the minds of those she served, her story a chapter in the university's rich history, a narrative of service and devotion.

The 1970s brought about significant social and technological changes, yet Ceil's role remained grounded in the timeless act of feeding and caring for others. Her experience at the University of Scranton during this era reflects a commitment that transcends time, a reminder of the human touch in education and the power of a community's collective memory to honor one of its own.

Unsung Pillars of the University of Scranton

3.127 Jean Schmidt
Cafeteria

In the fabric of the University of Scranton's history, some threads run quietly through its tapestry, unassuming yet indispensable. Jean Schmidt was one such thread in the 1970s, a cafeteria worker whose story is less about grand accolades and more about the daily bread of life and service.

Not much is known about Jean's past, where she came from, or the intricate details of her life before she joined the university staff. Yet, Jean found her role in the bustling world of the university cafeteria. She was part of a team that staffed the heart of the campus—a place where meals were as much about sustenance as warmth and a sense of belonging.

Although not documented for posterity, Jean's role would have been vital. Her days would have been filled with the early morning preparations of the dining area, the sorting of ingredients for the day's meals, and the serving of hundreds of students who came seeking nourishment for body and mind. The qualifications for such a role were less about formal education and more about the ability to serve with efficiency, kindness, and a steady hand.

The challenges of working in a university cafeteria during the 1970s were manifold. The lack of advanced technology meant everything was manual—from peeling vegetables to washing dishes. The pace was relentless, the work physically demanding, but it was fulfilling in its rhythm and routine.

Was Jean appreciated? One can imagine that in the hum of a satisfied dining hall, every thank you was a note in the symphony of her day's work. The management, fellow staff, and students—each interaction would have been a chance to be acknowledged, even in the most minor ways.

Her status among the people of Scranton was perhaps uncelebrated in the conventional sense. Still, those who relied on her service would have seen her as a pillar—a constant in their collegiate experience. Jean's feelings about working at the University of Scranton Catholic institution would have been personal. Still, one might speculate that the Catholic ethos of service and community informed her work and gave it meaning beyond the tasks.

Jean Schmidt's legacy is not etched in stone monuments but in the quieter remembrance of those she served—a legacy of reliability and the dignity of labor. She contributed to the university's narrative through loud achievements and the everyday grace of feeding the hungry. This role speaks volumes about the era and service ethos in its simplicity.

Her story mirrors the broader context of the 1970s, a time of social change and shifting norms, yet her work remained a constant within the university walls. Reflecting on that time and the evolution to today's technologically driven world, one can appreciate the timeless nature of her role and the impact of human connection that transcends decades, reminding us of the foundational importance of every role in an educational institution.

Unsung Pillars of the University of Scranton

Unsung Pillars of the University of Scranton

3.128 Betty Scholla
Treasurer's Office

Betty J. Sholla was a community weaver and a cultivator of generosity at the University of Scranton. Her journey at the institution began in 1959 in the Treasurer's Office, a world of figures and balance sheets. But it was in 1972 that she found her true calling in the realm of development and public relations, where she began to shape a legacy that would long outlive her tenure.

From the borough of Dunmore, Betty's life was steeped in the values of the Scranton community—resilience, faith, and a commitment to the common good. She compiled and maintained an operations manual, a testament to her meticulous nature and foresight, ensuring that the university's outreach efforts would be effective and enduring.

Betty's daily role as a development supervisor was a dance of strategy and stewardship. She operated the President's Club, orchestrating the annual Fund campaign with a conductor's precision. Her routines were less about repeating tasks and more about nurturing relationships—the kind that builds institutions.

Unsung Pillars of the University of Scranton

The work environment of the university was a tapestry of tradition and innovation. The Catholic identity of the institution was not just a backdrop but a cornerstone of the culture Betty helped to foster. It was a setting where values met action, and Betty's work embodied the university's mission.

The 1970s presented a unique set of challenges: technological limitations, economic shifts, and the need to engage a generation in the throes of change. Yet, Betty's triumphs were many, evidenced by the growth of the President's Club and the success of the Fund campaigns under her supervision.

Betty's relationships with co-workers, management, and students were founded on mutual respect and shared purpose. Her efforts were more than appreciated—they were integral to the university's progress. Her legacy is found in the scholarships funded, the facilities built, and the community strengthened through the campaigns she led.

In Scranton, Betty held a special place. Her work at a Catholic institution was not just a job but a vocation. Her status in the community was that of a quiet leader, someone whose impact was felt more than seen.

Betty passed away in 2014, leaving a legacy interwoven with the university's history. She is remembered for her dedication, strategic mind, and unwavering commitment to the university's mission. Her story is a chapter in the university's history that speaks of the transformative power of collective effort and the lasting impact of service.

Reflecting on the era in which she worked, Betty's experiences at the university during the 1970s were a microcosm of the broader societal shifts of the time. Her work stood as a bridge between the traditions of the past and the innovations that would define the future.

Betty J. Sholla's story is a tribute to those who serve behind the scenes, whose names may not always be known, but whose work creates the foundations for future generations. Her dedication to the University of Scranton is a beacon of the ethos of service that underpins education and community life. This ethos remains as vital today as it was in the era she served.

Unsung Pillars of the University of Scranton

3.129 Donna Scotchlas
Library

In the heart of Scranton, within the sturdy brick walls of the University's library, Donna Scotchlas found her calling amid the musty scent of books and the silent flutter of card catalogs. A daughter of the coal-strewn valleys of Pennsylvania, her roots delved as deep as the mineshafts, and her resilience was as unwavering as the steel tracks that laced the landscape. Scotchlas's journey to the library's hallowed halls was a ved by a quest for knowledge, a testament to her family's belief in the power of education.

As a cataloguer, Scotchlas was the invisible hand guiding students through a labyrinth of knowledge. Her days were rhythmed by the clack of the typewriter keys, coding each book with the promise of discovery. She found beauty in the Dewey Decimal System, her mind a living index of numbers and subjects. In a time untouched by digital ease, her role was arduous and indispensable, a bridge between inquiry and enlightenment.

The library, a bastion of academia, hummed with the undercurrent of intellectual pursuit. It was a place where the Catholic ethos subtly wove through the day-to-day; it was felt in the quiet respect for study, the communal quest for truth, and the shared reverence for the written word. Donna fit seamlessly into

Unsung Pillars of the University of Scranton

this tapestry, her work ethic mirroring the institution's values of diligence and service.

Challenges were manifold, from the analog conundrums of misfiled index cards to the continuous quest for space as volumes burgeoned. Budgets were tight, but Scotchlas's ingenuity stretched dollars and shelving to their limits. Her triumphs were the silent victories of order restored, of the rare book found, of the student's grateful nod.

Relationships in the workplace were cordial, a reflection of the times decorum. There was a kinship among the stacks, a shared mission that bound the staff. Management recognized her efforts with the nod of approval, while fellow librarians shared in the quiet pride of their collective labor. Students might not have known her name, but they knew the meticulous hand that organized their academic world.

In the quiet moments, Donna mused on her work. There was pride in her precision, satisfaction in the system's harmony, and a sense of fulfillment in the University's academic journey. The Catholic identity of the institution resonated with her, not in overt declarations of faith but in the commitment to a life of purpose and community.

Her impact was a whisper in the annals of the University's history, but those who knew knew well. The library, a nexus of learning, thrived partly due to her meticulous care. In the Scranton community, she was, among many, a quiet contributor to the city's fabric, her role perhaps unnoticed by the masses but vital within the University's microcosm.

Because of her dedication, Scotchlas's legacy lay in the order she left behind in the countless students who found their way

Unsung Pillars of the University of Scranton

through academic mazes. Like a bookmark in the pages of the institution's history, her memory marks the place of a bygone era.

The 1970s surrounded her with the spirit of change, yet within the library, time stood still, preserving the essence of scholarly pursuit. Today, the digitized world would scarcely recognize the labor of her days. The role of religion in education, the respect for quiet labor, and the pace of academic life have all shifted. Yet, Scotchlas's story remains a narrative of constancy and commitment in an ever-changing world.

Unsung Pillars of the University of Scranton

3.130 Frank Shutkufski
Maintenance Supervisor

In the heart of Scranton, amidst the bustle of university life and the calm of sacred halls, a man worked whose hands had shaped more than just the physical landscape. Frank, a widower with the gentle demeanor of a practiced carpenter, carried his toolbox with the ease of decades. A veteran of war and life's unpredictable storms, he had seen the world outside before returning to the arms of his hometown. Frank's story was not one penned in the annals of the famous or the mighty; it was written in the everyday, the ordinary, and the spaces between.

Joining the University of Scranton in the vibrant but challenging era of the 1970s, Frank's role as a maintenance supervisor was anything but mundane. He was the unseen heartbeat of the campus, ensuring the hum of machinery and the integrity of structures. His days were spent in the company of wrenches and blueprints, walking the grounds he knew like the back of his weathered hand. The Johnson Institute of Technology alum and Army veteran brought a meticulous eye to the university, an eye honed by years of union carpentry and construction superintendence.

But what of the man behind the maintenance? Frank was a soul rooted in community, from the Veterans of Foreign Wars to the Holy Name Society of Saint Joseph's church. He found solace in the stillness of fishing, a respite from the noise of his daily toils. His devotion to his daughters, church, and Ukrainian heritage spoke of a life rich with connection and tradition.

His work, often unseen, was not unacknowledged. Students may not have known his name, but they felt the warmth of buildings in winter and the cool respite of shade from well-placed trees, his silent gifts to them. Colleagues respected his steadfastness, and management relied on his unwavering competence. Yet, in the quiet of the maintenance shed, one might catch a glimpse of satisfaction in Frank's eyes, a testament to his pride in his craft.

The Catholic spirit of the institution was not lost on him. It was a balm to his grieving heart, a familiar embrace in a rapidly changing world. His faith, intertwined with his work, was evident in the respect he showed to every person and every task. In a time of social upheaval, Frank's steadfast presence was as comforting as the church bells that marked the hours.

Frank's legacy is not one of grandeur but of permanence. The trees he planted offer shade, the benches he repaired still hold conversations, and the doors he hung open to the future. His story reminds us of the dignity of labor, community strength, and the enduring power of service. Buried in Saint Joseph's Cemetery, Frank rests among those he served, his life a testament to the lasting impact of a job well done. In Scranton, he remains a symbol of the era he helped shape, his memory etched not in stone but in the lives he touched.

Unsung Pillars of the University of Scranton

3.131 William Shutkufski
Carpenter

In a time of change, William Shutkufski carried the legacy of an era on his shoulders, hammering away at the future one nail at a time. Hailing from a modest upbringing, he found his rhythm early on, his hands as adept at shaping wood as his mind was at solving problems. Valedictorian of the Johnson Institute of Technology class of 1931, William wasn't just skilled; he was a craftsman who knew the soul of wood.

As a master carpenter and a pillar of the Carpenters Union, William brought more than just his toolbox to the University of Scranton. He got a dedication that was almost sacramental. The university's Gothic arches and red brick walls stood testament to the hands that toiled — not just for a paycheck, but for a purpose. William's role transcended mere maintenance; he was a curator of an educational edifice, ensuring the institution stood robust for minds eager to learn.

His days would start with the smell of sawdust, a material as humble as he, ye central to the grand structures he maintained and improved. William found a meditative peace in the clamor of power saws and the silence of precise measurements. It wasn't just about fixing broken benches or crafting new podiums; it was about shaping an environment conducive to pursuing knowledge.

The 1970s brought challenges — budgets were tight, and the technology was far from today's capabilities. Yet, William navigated these constraints with ingenuity and a resourceful spirit. His triumphs may not have made headlines, but they echoed in the quiet corners of the campus, where students and staff benefited from his work.

At Saint Joseph's Church, he was a familiar face, his faith as much a part of his craft. And though his contributions were often behind the scenes, the respect he garnered was palpable. He wasn't just maintaining buildings; he was upholding a tradition, a Catholic ethos that permeated his work.

His rapport with fellow staff, management, and students was marked by a quiet respect — a mutual acknowledgment of the small but essential cogs that keep the grand machinery of an institution running. Was his work appreciated? William found his answer in the nods of professors, in the gratitude of students who might not know his name but knew the comfort of the spaces he maintained.

William's view of his role was devoid of pretension. Working at a Catholic institution meant being part of a continuum of service and humility. He saw his work as a vocation, not just a job. It was his way of contributing to a greater good — the education of generations.

His legacy is not in grand monuments but in the minutiae of maintenance logs and the silent prayers of a job well done. He is remembered in the echoes of cathedral halls, the sturdy desks

Unsung Pillars of the University of Scranton

that bore the weight of countless textbooks, and the memories of those who knew the quiet dignity of his labor.

William's story is a thread in Scranton's history, reflecting the dynamic, faith-driven community. His impact on the University of Scranton was subtle but substantial, a testament to the idea that every role, no matter how seemingly small, is a cornerstone in the edifice of education.

In today's digitized, fast-paced world, we look back at William's era with nostalgia. The 1970s were a time of analog craftsmanship, where the tactile connection between hand and material was intimate. William's time at the university reminds us of a period when religion and education were deeply intertwined, providing a foundation that, while evolving, still underpins the institution's values to this day.

William Shutkufski, a carpenter, a family man, a community member, and a quiet guardian of a future he knew he would not see but was helping to build, one day at a time.

Unsung Pillars of the University of Scranton

3.132 Stephanie Silvestri
Graduate Office

Stephanie Silvestri might not have graced the headlines. Still, in the heart of Scranton, within the hallowed halls of the University, she was a beacon of progression in an era of transformation. With little known about her beginnings, Stephanie's story at the graduate office during the early 1970s speaks volumes of the uncelebrated heroism in the mundane.

She was the unseen metronome of the institution, her duties likely encompassing the orchestration of graduate affairs — from the meticulous filing of records to the delicate handling of student queries. Each task, while seemingly pedestrian, was a vital stitch in the academic tapestry of the University of Scranton.

The graduate office was no place for the faint-hearted. The 1970s were times of burgeoning technological change, yet still tethered to analog traditions. Budgets were lean, and the demands were high. Stephanie's days were likely a juggling act of paperwork and people — the lifeblood of a graduate office that aspired to maintain academic excellence amidst the kinetic energy of post-secondary education.

In an institution where Catholic values were more than just a backdrop, they infused the essence of work and community. For Stephanie, this would have meant working within a culture of service and morality, her role an unspoken sermon of dedication.

Unsung Pillars of the University of Scranton

Difficulties were part of the daily grind. The era was not kind to the keepers of records and schedules; the digital ease we know today was a distant future. Yet, the triumphs were in the details — a successfully coordinated thesis defense, a timetable that miraculously accommodated all, and a student's grateful smile after a session of guidance.

Relationships in the workplace, especially within the microcosm of a university department, are the silent narratives that texture our careers. For Stephanie, camaraderie with colleagues, the respect of management, and the affection of students would have been the accurate measure of her success. While not etched in stone, her legacy lived in the memories of those she aided and the systems she helped establish.

Her contributions to the University of Scranton would have been subtle yet profound, like the quiet confidence of a nun in prayer, knowing that her efforts were a part of something greater. Her pride in her work was likely akin to the silent pride of a city built on coal — resilient, enduring, and foundational.

The community of Scranton, a tapestry of working-class ethos and Catholic values, likely saw Stephanie as one of their own — a figure who contributed not just to the academia but to the very spirit of the community. Outside the University, while undocumented, her role in the community would have been interwoven with the cultural and social fabric of the city.

Stephanie's story is not just a memory; it is a testament to women's silent but essential roles in a time when their contributions were often overshadowed. As the University marches on into the future, the echoes of her work still resonate in the administrative practices, the culture of support, and the unspoken history of those who serve without fanfare.

Unsung Pillars of the University of Scranton

Reflecting on the 1970s, one sees a period of both constraint and possibility. Working at a Catholic institution then, Stephanie would have been at the intersection of tradition and change. Today, her story is a bridge to an era when the role of religion in education was more pronounced, and technology was just beginning to redefine the academic landscape.

Stephanie Silvestri, a name that may not be known to all, played her part in the grand narrative of the University of Scranton. In doing so, she left an indelible mark on the fabric of an institution that continues to weave the future from the threads of the past.

Unsung Pillars of the University of Scranton

3.133 Michael Size
Cafeteria

In the bustling halls of the University of Scranton's cafeteria in the early 1970s, you could find Michael Size, a figure as constant as the institution itself. His origins were modest; he was a local son of Scranton with roots deeply embedded in the Pennsylvania soil. Education had been a luxury, not a given, for Michael, and the university job was a stroke of luck after high school—a chance to stay close to home while earning a living.

As a cafeteria employee, Michael's role was pivotal yet unpretentious. His days were a symphony of routine tasks: stocking supplies, operating the food stations, and ensuring the stainless steel counters gleamed. The hum of refrigerators and the clatter of trays served as his daily soundtrack. This was a time when technology was rudimentary, and hands did most of the work. Despite the repetitive nature of his duties, Michael found satisfaction in the order he brought to the chaos of a college dining hall.

The work environment was a crucible of academic enthusiasm and Catholic traditions. The university's identity was palpable in the halls Michael walked; it was a place where faith met education, a combination that seemed to bring a sense of community to all who worked there. A practicing Catholic,

Unsung Pillars of the University of Scranton

Michael felt a kinship with the institution's values, and this connection fueled his diligence.

Challenges were part of the job—the occasional shortage of supplies, the unending influx of hungry students, and the wear and tear on equipment. Yet, Michael's triumphs were the small victories: the successful lunch rush, the newly implemented food station, and the gratitude of a student nourished for their studies.

In terms of interpersonal relationships, Michael was a thread in the fabric of the university community. His rapport with fellow staff was built on mutual respect, and management knew him as reliable, a silent guardian of the students' sustenance. Students might not have known him by name, but they recognized his face, his steady presence a comforting part of their college experience.

Michael's reflections on his work were a tapestry of pride and contentment. There was frustration in moments of exhaustion, but a greater sense of fulfillment overshadowed these. He saw his role as a supporting beam in the grand structure of the university, helping to uphold the institution's mission to educate and nurture.

His impact was subtle but significant. While not the recipient of grand accolades, Michael's dedication did not go unnoticed. A nod from a professor, a smile from a student, an extra day of leave granted by management—these were his badges of appreciation.

Michael's job was not glamorous in Scranton, but was respected. As an employee of the university, he was seen as a contributor to the city's intellectual and spiritual life. His presence at church on

Unsung Pillars of the University of Scranton

Sundays and his volunteer work at local food drives wove him into the community's tapestry beyond the university's walls.

Michael's legacy was not recorded in history books. Still, it lived on in the memories of those who knew him, the smooth cafeteria operation, and the alums who might recall the man who served them during their formative years. His legacy was one of dedication and quiet service.

The 1970s were a time of change, and though the university seemed a world apart, the era's social currents flowed through its campus. Economic strains, cultural shifts, and political upheaval touched the lives of all Americans, including those in the quiet city of Scranton.

Reflecting on that era from today's vantage point, the contrast is stark. Working in a Catholic institution then was to be enveloped in a community with a shared identity. Now, technology, shifting social norms, and the evolving role of religion in education have transformed the landscape dramatically. Yet, at the heart of it, the essence of work like Michael's remains the same—a commitment to service, community, and the common good.

3.134 Elaine Smerecky
Alumni Office

Elaine Smerecky, with roots deep in the coal-rich earth of Scranton, emerged from the humble heart of the city. Her background was a tapestry of local lore and familial dedication, a narrative shared by the tight-knit communities of Pennsylvania. Her education was a testament to her determination, with each step leading her closer to an institution she would come to serve and shape.

In the early 1970s, Elaine found her place within the walls of the University of Scranton, not as a student but as a beacon in the alum office. Her days were spent amidst the hum of typewriters and the rustle of records, the heartbeat of past pupils pulsing through her daily tasks. As an alum officer, her role was to bridge the gap between generations, a custodian of connections who ensured that the graduates remained a part of their alma mater's evolving story.

The work environment was a blend of academia and faith, where the Catholic identity of the institution was not merely a backdrop but a living, breathing aspect of everyday life. It subtly influenced Elaine's work, from the values that underscored her interactions to the spirit of service that defined her duties.

Unsung Pillars of the University of Scranton

Challenges were not scarce, with the era's technological limitations requiring a meticulousness that today's digital age seldom demands. Budget constraints often meant doing more with less, yet Elaine triumphed in creating events and programs that kept the alums engaged and invested. Her successes were quiet but profound, laying the groundwork for traditions that would outlive her tenure.

Elaine's relationships in the office were the sinews that held her work together. The camaraderie with co-workers was her support system; the management's trust in her was unwavering, and students, often on the cusp of becoming alums themselves, saw in her a future friend. Conflicts were rare, but when they arose, Elaine navigated them with the grace and wisdom of a seasoned diplomat.

Her reflections on her work were a mix of pride and humility. The job was more than a means to an end—it was a calling. She found fulfillment in knowing that her efforts contributed to the university's mission, which sought to educate and foster a community for life.

Elaine's impact was like ripples on the surface of a lake, her efforts recognized in the letters of thanks from alums, the acknowledgments at gatherings, and the occasional, much-cherished commendation from the university's hierarchy.

Within Scranton, Elaine's role was that of an unsung hero. Her job might not have been in the public eye, but her involvement in church and community initiatives linked her to the city's fabric. She was a familiar face synonymous with the university's commitment to community service.

Unsung Pillars of the University of Scranton

Elaine's legacy is not etched in stone monuments but in the living legacy of relationships she fostered. It is in the network of alums who continue to contribute to the university, in the events that still gather crowds, and in the ethos of the alum office that she helped to shape.

The 1970s were times of transformation, and while Elaine's work was within the university's Catholic haven, the era's spirit of change did not pass her by. It was when tradition met progress, shaping her role and approach to her work.

Looking back, working in a Catholic institution in that era was to be part of a community with a shared mission, contrasting to today's more secular, technologically-driven approach. Yet, Elaine's story is a reminder that regardless of the decade, the essence of commitment to one's community and values remains timeless.

3.135 Anthony Smoleski
Painter

In the heart of Scranton, within the walls of the University, a story was etched in the colors that only Anthony Smoleski could mix on his palette. Born and bred in the coal city, Tony, as he was fondly called, carried the humility of the town in his gait and the diligence in his hands. He was a fabric of the local tapestry, an army veteran who had stories of the Pacific in his eyes, which perhaps only the walls he painted could retell.

Tony joined the University of Scranton in the early '70s, a time of change and vigor, with his role as a painter defining more than just the aesthetics of the campus. His brush strokes were like the silent narrators of the University's evolving chapters. Each corridor he painted, every wall he restored, echoed the Catholic spirit of the institution, a silent oath to maintain not just the physical but the spiritual scaffold of the place.

His days would start with the sun as he pushed his cart through the halls, greeting the echoing footsteps of early risers. The scent of fresh paint was a testament to his presence, a mark of progress and care. The job was never easy; working with old buildings demanded patience and an almost artisanal touch, which Tony had mastered over the years. There was pride in his work, a

Unsung Pillars of the University of Scranton

sense of satisfaction in preserving the University's legacy, a feeling that was palpable to anyone who walked by his fresh canvases.

The community at the University, a mosaic of students, faculty, and fellow staff, appreciated Tony's quiet dedication. His was a familiar face that didn't demand attention but was always acknowledged with a nod, a smile, or a wave. He was part of the University's rhythm, a consistent, reliable beat in the background music of academia.

Tony's legacy wasn't just in the layers of paint he left behind but in how he upheld the institution's values. Even as a layperson in a Catholic university, he represented the inclusivity and acceptance that the '70s were inching towards. The university walls held his confessions of war and peace, his hopes for the future, and his love for the game of bowling, which he often joked was as much about precision as his daily work.

The community of Scranton, a town as tight-knit as the bristles on his brushes, held Tony in high regard. His role at the University was a badge of honor, reflecting the city's hard work and reverence ethos. Even beyond the campus, he was known as the man who 'painted' the town's youth with the colors of knowledge and respect.

In Saint Joseph's cemetery lies Anthony Smoleski, a man whose life was a mural of service. His story, intertwined with the history of the University, the city of Scranton, and the tides of the 1970s, stands as a reminder of the silent architects of our spaces, the quiet custodians of our heritage. His work, his ethos, and the respect he garnered are the hues that will color the University's narrative for generations to come.

3.136 Jacob Snyder
Saint Thomas Hall

Though worn and lined with the years, Jacob Snyder's hands held a steadiness that spoke of unwavering dedication. Born to the coal-stained streets of Scranton, Jacob's life was as much a part of this town as the anthracite that runs beneath it. A graduate of Saint Mary's High, he carried the values of his alma mater into every crevice of his life, mainly so after the untimely passing of his wife left him a widower with children to raise on the humble earnings of a maintenance man.

The University of Scranton's Saint Thomas Hall knew Jacob's footsteps well; after all, he joined the staff in 1961 and trod its corridors for two decades. His role was as essential as it was unseen, ensuring the hum of the campus's heart never missed a beat. From the roar of the heating systems to the silent flicker of a replaced bulb, Jacob's hands wove the tapestry of campus life, largely unnoticed but deeply felt.

In those early '70s, the world outside was a whirlwind of change, but Jacob found solace in the steady rhythm of his duties within Saint Thomas Hall. The Catholic identity of the university was a silent companion to his day-to-day tasks, a reminder of the service beyond self that his role embodied. Yet, it was in 1981 that the university acknowledged his silent vigil through the

Unsung Pillars of the University of Scranton

years, bestowing upon him the 'Pro Deo Et Universitate' — for God and University — an honor that echoed his unspoken credo.

The challenges were many — antiquated equipment, tight budgets, and the ever-present demand for more hands than the university could employ. But Jacob's satisfaction lay not in the ease of the work but in the necessity of it. His triumphs were the avoided crises, the comfort preserved for the educated youth who may never know his name but knew the warmth of well-kept halls.

His camaraderie with fellow staff was a mosaic of shared lunches and mutual grumbles over broken machinery. Management knew him as dependable, the students as a fixture as reliable as the sunrise. His presence was a gentle reassurance, an embodiment of the constancy of the institution itself.

Jacob's role was modest in the broader Scranton community, yet his impact was significant. The university's standing as a beacon of education and faith was, in part, upheld by his diligent service. He was one of their own to the local community, representing their collective hard work and devotion ethic.

Retirement did little to fade the legacy of Jacob Snyder. His legacy is not etched in stone but in the lived experience of the institution. The creak-free floors, the windows that held back winter's chill, and the doors that opened smoothly for thousands of students are testaments to his service.

Reflecting upon his time, Jacob might have seen the university as a microcosm of the era's shifts. The '70s brought upheaval, but within the campus's Catholic embrace, Jacob found a continuity that anchored him. Working in such an institution was to be a silent guardian of tradition in an age of flux.

Today, Saint Thomas Hall is a monument to education, and Jacob Snyder's life reminds us that every brick laid in earnest upholds the cathedral of learning. As Scranton continues to evolve, the memory of Jacob's service endures, a subtle reminder that the proper foundations of any great institution are often the hands that tend it, quietly and without fanfare.

Unsung Pillars of the University of Scranton

3.137 Ruth Snyder
Treasurer's Office

In the echoing halls of the University of Scranton's Treasury Office, where the pulse of financial life thrummed steadily, Ruth Farley Snyder held the strings tight. Her journey had begun in the heart of Scranton itself, raised in the warmth of John and Mary O'Boyle Farley's home, molded by the city's schools, and eventually blossoming into a guardian of numbers and cents at the University.

A title such as 'Payroll Manager' scarcely justifies Ruth's role in those brisk, early 1970s mornings. She was the unseen hand that guided the livelihood of countless educators and staff, a silent sentinel ensuring every dollar was accounted for and every paycheck delivered with precision. The Catholic spirit of the institution was more than just a backdrop; the ethical compass directed her meticulous work.

The University was a tapestry of the era's hopes and challenges, with Ruth woven inextricably into its fabric. She faced the daily rigors of an evolving administrative landscape, where the analog gave grudging way to the digital, and every technological leap was a chasm she crossed with determination.

Unsung Pillars of the University of Scranton

Her colleagues and the students whose lives she unknowingly touched formed a mosaic of interactions. There were shared smiles over coffee breaks, nods of gratitude from professors, and the quiet satisfaction of a job well done. Ruth's labor was a foundation stone in the bustling academic citadel, often unheralded but deeply felt.

Despite the confines of her office, Ruth's essence spilled out into Scranton, echoing the community's hardworking spirit. Intertwined with her vocational duties, her Catholic faith lent her a sense of service that transcended the University's walls.

As the years unfurled and Ruth traded the snows of Scranton for the sun of Bradenton, she left behind more than just ledgers and balance sheets. Her legacy, etched in the countless lives made smoother by her diligence, remains a testament to the quiet heroes of the workplace. To the University, she was a steward of resources; to her family, a beacon of love and strength; and to Scranton, one of its own, whose work resonated far beyond the echo of the closing office door.

Now, as the memory of Ruth Farley Snyder is cradled in the private sanctity of Cathedral Cemetery, one can't help but reflect on how the simplicity of her tasks belied their actual impact. Ruth's constancy was a rare treasure in a decade marked by upheaval and change. And while the world outside transformed, her dedication was a steady flame, illuminating the path for those who followed in her footsteps.

Unsung Pillars of the University of Scranton

3.138 Mary Spellman
Academic Vice-President's Office

In the bustling corridors of the University of Scranton, amidst the whirl of youthful ambition and academic pursuit, Mary W. Spellman was a steadfast presence. A mother of four, her journey to the heart of this Catholic institution was paved with diligence and a penchant for service, hallmarks of her time as a secretary in the office of the academic vice president during the early 1970s.

Coming from the close-knit fabric of Scranton, Mary's roots ran as deep as the coal mines encircling the city. Educated at Saint John's School and Lackawanna Junior College, she brought her academic credentials and the warmth of a family woman to the stately office she helped run. Before her university tenure, Mary honed her organizational acumen as a secretary for the Murray Corporation, serving through the tumult of World War II and the reconfiguration of American industry that followed.

At the university, Mary's role was as much about managing schedules and correspondence as it was about being the unseen hand that steadied the ship. Her tasks ranged from the mundane to the monumental, often acting as a conduit between the administration and the student body. The clack of her typewriter was a metronome to academic life, producing memos, minutes, and manuscripts under the watchful eye of the vice president.

The challenges were many—technological limitations meant everything was done by hand or with primary machines. Budget constraints often require creative solutions to administrative problems. Yet, Mary found triumph in every task completed, every event successfully organized, and every student or faculty member helped. Her dedication earned her the Pro Deo et Universitate award, a testament to her years of unwavering commitment to the institution.

Relationships were the bedrock of Mary's career. She was known for her capacity to listen, advise, and mediate when necessary. Her office was a sanctuary for those needing guidance or simply a moment of respite from the demands of academia. She was respected by her peers and cherished by students who saw in her a figure of constancy and care.

The Catholic identity of the university no doubt shaped the fabric of Mary's workplace. In an era of societal upheaval and the quest for personal freedoms, the institution stood as a bastion of traditional values, with faith interwoven into the educational tapestry. Mary, with her deep-seated faith, found harmony between her work and her spiritual life, each reinforcing the other.

Her legacy within the university is etched not in stone but in the hearts of those she touched. While a physical recognition, the Pro Deo et Universitate award pales compared to the collective memory of her kindness and efficiency. Beyond the campus, in Scranton itself, Mary was a testament to women's role in supporting and shaping educational institutions during a change.

Unsung Pillars of the University of Scranton

The 1970s, with its shifting social and economic landscapes, was a backdrop to Mary's tenure at the university. Her story, interlaced with the narratives of women's burgeoning roles in the workplace, the evolution of secretarial work, and the steady hand of Catholic education during a period of transformation, offers a window into an era that set the stage for progress to come.

Mary W. Spellman, with her typewriter, her awards, and her gentle influence, is remembered not just for the tasks she accomplished but for the lives she enriched. Her work at the University of Scranton is a reminder of how personal dedication can resonate through an institution, shaping its course and touching the future of one student, one faculty member, and one challenge at a time.

3.139 Barbara Spencer
Faculty Offices

Barbara Spencer arrived at the University of Scranton with the quiet determination that characterized the women of her time. Her roots were modest, her education solid—enough to navigate the responsibilities that would greet her at the faculty offices. In the early 1970s, she entered the university's halls as a secretary, a role that belied the juggling act she would perform daily.

Barbara's job title hardly captured the full scope of her duties. She was the unseen engine in the academic machine, typing memos on her IBM Selectric, answering calls on a rotary phone, and managing schedules with a precision that the era's technology scarcely allowed. Her tasks were as varied as they were vital, from ensuring that faculty meetings ran smoothly to deciphering handwritten notes into formal correspondence.

The work environment of the University of Scranton was stoic and serene, echoing the Catholic values it upheld. Barbara found her place amid stacks of paper and the rhythmic clacking of typewriter keys. The Catholic identity of the institution was a silent partner in every interaction, shaping the decorum with which every conversation was held, and every decision was made.

Challenges were as frequent as they were formidable. The limited technology meant every document needed careful

Unsung Pillars of the University of Scranton

planning; there was no 'delete' key for mistakes. Budget constraints were a constant balancing act, requiring a frugality that Barbara managed gracefully. Yet, she thrived, her triumphs often unnoticed but integral to the academic fabric.

Interpersonal relationships in such a setting were a delicate dance of professionalism and humanity. Barbara was a confidant to some and a silent ally to others. Her interactions were marked by a mutual respect that crossed the lines between staff, faculty, and students. She was the one who remembered birthdays, who listened to the worries of a homesick freshman, who smoothed the ruffled feathers of tenured professors.

The job was not without frustrations, but Barbara's reflections were often laced with pride. She saw her work as a contribution to the university's larger mission—to educate and to guide. To her, every letter typed, every meeting arranged, was a brick laid in the foundation of someone's future.

Her impact was like a whisper that moved through the halls, seldom acknowledged with awards but deeply felt in the seamless day-to-day operations of the university. Management knew her worth, as did the students who left her office a little more assured than when they entered.

Barbara's role within the Scranton community extended beyond the university gates. Her job was a testament to the work ethic admired by the townspeople, a reflection of the city's spirit. While she may not have held a public position, her influence was felt in the quiet support she provided to local events and causes.

Today, Barbara's legacy is not enshrined in plaques or statues but in the collective memory of those she touched—a courteous nod from a former student and a grateful smile from a retired professor. Her story is a thread in the tapestry of the university's history, one of countless others that form the institution's heritage.

The 1970s were a time of change, and the social and political tides of the era certainly lapped at the edges of Barbara's world. Yet, her story is a reminder of the constancy of dedication and the timeless value of support.

Reflecting on her time at a Catholic institution during those years, one might ponder the contrasts with today. The technology has evolved, the social norms have shifted, and the role of religion in education is ever-changing. Yet, the essence of Barbara's work—a commitment to service and community—remains as relevant now as it was then.

Unsung Pillars of the University of Scranton

3.140 James Talerico
Estate

In the early 1970s, nestled within the Jesuit Estate of the University of Scranton, there worked a person whose daily toil threaded through the fabric of academic life yet whose story remained largely untold—James Talerico, a name not etched in the grand halls of academia but inscribed in the quieter corners of diligent service.

Talerico hailed from a modest background, with roots that traced through the coal-dusted heartlands of Pennsylvania. His family, steeped in the values of hard work and education, saw young James navigate his way to the gates of the University of Scranton, not as a scholar but as a steward of the campus grounds.

As a custodian of the Jesuit Estate, James's responsibilities were as varied as the seasons. His days were a symphony of routine and unexpected tasks—polishing the woodwork that lined the estate's library, ensuring the gardens mirrored the meticulousness of scholarly thought, and attending to the repairs whispered by aging infrastructure. It was a role that demanded reverence for tradition and the skill to adapt to the institution's evolving needs.

The university's physical environment was a testament to its Catholic identity—a crucible where faith and reason coexisted.

Unsung Pillars of the University of Scranton

Talerico's work was a silent sermon that underscored the Jesuit maxim of finding God in all things. Whether setting up for mass or preparing the estate for academic festivities, his role was a bridge between the sacred and the scholarly.

Challenges were no strangers to James. The early '70s bore the marks of economic strain and the technological infancy that preceded the digital age. Yet, through ingenuity and perseverance, he maintained the integrity of the university's physical narrative. His triumphs were not those sung at commencements but felt in the seamless flow of daily campus life.

Talerico's rapport with others was the kind that underpins any community—unassuming yet fundamental. His interactions with faculty, students, and fellow staff wove a tapestry of mutual respect and shared purpose. Acknowledgment came not always in awards but in nods of appreciation, the kind that recognizes the quiet dignity of keeping the wheels turning.

In Scranton, James was both a spectator and a participant. His role at the university was a silent thread in the city's larger tapestry, reflective of the community's values and relationship with the institution—a man whose work was a subtle yet constant presence.

The legacy of James Talerico, while not encapsulated in plaques or statues, lives in the alma mater's continued vibrancy. It is in the way the estate still stands, proud and pristine—a testament to the countless, unseen moments of care.

The epoch of the '70s wrapped around Talerico's tenure like the ivy on university walls. It was a time of social upheaval and change, yet his dedication was a steadying force within the estate's confines, a reminder of the enduring values amidst the world's churn.

Reflecting on the era, one might muse on how a university custodian's quiet yet pivotal role would evolve with the advent of technology and shifting societal norms. Yet, the essence of Talerico's contribution—to serve with humility and resilience—remains timeless, a narrative as relevant today as it was in the era of his stewardship.

Unsung Pillars of the University of Scranton

Unsung Pillars of the University of Scranton

3.141 Stanley Tavieski
Cafeteria

Stanley Tavieski, a name not widely known yet woven into the fabric of the University of Scranton's history, hails from a modest family background. Like many of his generation, his education was not a litany of degrees but a testament to life's hard knocks and the school of experience. When the early 1970s ushered him into the university's cafeteria, it was an abrupt entry into a role that would mark his legacy.

Assigned the humble title of Cafeteria Employee, Stanley's days were rhythmed by the clatter of trays and the symphony of student voices. His responsibilities were manifold - serving meals, maintaining cleanliness, and perhaps, most importantly, being the unseen pillar supporting the daily hustle of university life. Unique to his time, he may have managed tasks without today's technology, ensuring each student was nourished by food and kindness.

The Catholic identity of the University of Scranton was the invisible thread in the tapestry of Stanley's work environment. It created a culture of community and service that Stanley embraced, adding his thread to the weave with quiet dedication.

Yet, the job was not without its trials. The era was not kind to those in service roles, often unseen and unsung. But Stanley

Unsung Pillars of the University of Scranton

faced these challenges with a resilience that spoke of a more profound satisfaction - pride in being a cog in the wheel of the greater good of the institution.

His rapport with others was the stuff of everyday magic - the shared nods with co-workers, the grateful smiles from students, the respectful exchanges with management. Each interaction, a stitch in the fabric of communal life, each day, a tapestry richer for his presence.

In personal reflections, one might imagine a man of few words finding fulfillment in the routine, taking pride in the essential nature of his work. Stanley's view of his role in the catholic institution might have been grounded in a personal faith mirrored in his service.

Appreciation for Stanley's efforts was a quiet affair. Perhaps there were no awards, but the smooth running of the cafeteria, the student's satisfaction, and his peers' respect were accolades enough.

In the broader community of Scranton, Stanley's role might have seemed insignificant to some, but to those who knew the university's pulse, he was a steadfast sentinel of student welfare. Though not superb, his job was essential to the university's daily life and, by extension, to the city that housed it.

Stanley's legacy is not in the annals of history books but in the collective memory of those he served. He left an indelible mark on the institution, a reminder that every role, no matter how small, is crucial.

The 1970s were a time of change, and working in a Catholic institution then involved navigating a world where tradition met

Unsung Pillars of the University of Scranton

the tidal wave of modernity. Stanley's experiences were a microcosm of this, his story a single note in the era's complex melody.

Today, reflecting on Stanley's time at the University of Scranton, one sees the contrast of an era less connected, yet perhaps more intimately bound by shared daily experiences, a time when the human touch was not an option but the essence of every job

3.142 Mary Terrinoni
Language Laboratory

Mary A. Terrinoni, a pillar of constancy in the flux of academia, began her journey at the University of Scranton as a fresh-faced secretary in the wintry breath of January 1957. Her roots ran deep through Scranton's soil, a native whose life would weave through the city's tapestry as intricately as the lace of the altar cloths in the town's cathedral.

She rose through the ranks with the quiet dignity of the unassuming, her daily march through the halls marked by the click-clack symphony of a manual typewriter. By 1957, she had become the right hand to the Academic Vice President, serving as a gatekeeper and an unsung architect of the college's burgeoning arts and science programs.

The university's corridors whispered with her diligence, her presence a comforting constant amidst the brief tenure of students and faculty. In the language laboratory, she reigned for a decade, her fingers dancing over the keys, translating the babble of tongues into order and structure.

Her ascent to a senior position in 1973 was a personal triumph and a testament to the silent yet steadfast women who prop up the towers of education. The university recognized her servitude with the Pro Deo Et Universitate award—a nod often reserved for the luminaries of academia, yet none more deserving than she.

But it was not just the university that benefited from Mary's dedication. Mercy Hospital in Scranton knew her, too, as the volunteer whose generosity with time was as boundless as her capacity for work.

The Catholic identity of the institution was a silent rhythm to her workday, a cadence that aligned with her moral compass. Her duties, though often behind the scenes, were crucial cogs in the wheel of the university's daily life—scheduling, organizing, and facilitating the unseen logistics that are the lifeblood of any institution.

Her challenges were many—technological limitations of the 1970s, the ceaseless demand for efficiency in an era before digital convenience—but she met them with the same quiet resolve that characterized her persona.

As for the community of Scranton, she was one of their own, embodying the values that held them together. She was a mirror of their work ethic, a reflection of their spirit. Her role extended beyond the university, touching the lives of those who never set foot on campus yet felt the ripple of her impact through her volunteer work and presence in the city.

Upon her retirement to Berks County, she carried with her not just the memories but the essence of a career that was as much a vocation as it was a job. She passed away in 2014, leaving behind a legacy etched not in stone but in the lives of those she touched—a legacy that rests not only in the Immaculate Conception Cemetery but in the annals of the University of Scranton, memorable and enduring.

Unsung Pillars of the University of Scranton

In the 1970s, Mary's story unfolded in a time of social upheaval, yet within the hallowed halls of the Catholic institution, she found a sanctum of purpose and pride. Her story reflects not just her era but a bridge to our own, reminding us that while the world changes, the essence of commitment and service remains timeless.

3.143 Alfred Thomas
Student Center

In the heart of Scranton, amid the hustle of academic life and the calm of sacred halls, Alfred L. Thomas moved like an unseen current, keeping the lifeblood of the University of Scranton flowing. From the coal-dusted valleys of South Wales, where his life began, to the bread ovens of his youth, where he toiled as a baker, Alfred's journey was as textured as the crust of his loaves. War called, and he answered, serving with quiet courage in the crucible of World War II.

Returning home, a family man now, he sought the peace that had eluded him in the trenches, finding solace in the serene rituals of maintenance work. Alfred's days at the University of Scranton were a tapestry of routine and responsibility, his hands ensuring the Student Center stood as a testament to the community it served. His role, often invisible to the untrained eye, was vital — a guardian of the institution's heartbeat.

The Student Center, a crossroads of young aspirations and scholarly pursuit, was his charge, and he approached it with the precision of a craftsman. The clang of heating pipes, the hum of polished floors, and the sparkle of cleaned windows were verses in his unsung symphony. His days were a blend of the mechanical and the mundane, tasks that required a steadfast hand and a keen eye for detail.

Unsung Pillars of the University of Scranton

The University, with its Catholic identity, was not just a workplace but a community where faith and education were intertwined, and Alfred, though not overtly religious, respected this sanctity. He saw the reflection of his values in the institution — hard work, dedication, and a commitment to family and community.

Challenge was no stranger to him. The era's technological simplicity demanded more sweat and sinew and fewer switches and buttons. Budgets were tight, but Alfred's ingenuity was tighter still, finding solutions where others saw problems. His triumphs were the unnoticed disasters averted, the crises calmly contained.

He was a quiet force among peers, acknowledged with nods and the knowing smiles of shared toil. Students passed him in hallways, oblivious to the man whose labor allowed their academic pursuits to thrive unimpeded. Management appreciated him in the pragmatic way of institutions, through the lens of function and necessity.

In Scranton, a town built on the back of industry and community spirit, Alfred held a place of unspoken respect. His role at the University made him a custodian of a vital community pillar, his contributions extending beyond the campus to the very fabric of the town.

Alfred's legacy lies in the corridors he walked, the machinery he maintained, and the lives he indirectly touched. He is remembered in the quiet gratitude of a job well done, a presence felt in absence, a story woven into the University's history.

Unsung Pillars of the University of Scranton

The 1970s enveloped Alfred in a world teetering on change, his narrative intersecting with the shifting tides of societal norms, the emergence of new technologies, and the evolving role of religion in public life. Had they been recorded, his reflections might have spoken to the constancy of change, the enduring need for the work of one's hands, and the timeless value of service.

In the hallowed grounds of Fairview Memorial Park, Alfred rests, his story etched in stone and memory. Though silent as the grave, his life's work echoes in the hallowed halls of the institution he served, a testament to the enduring power of dedication and the quiet heroism of the everyday.

Unsung Pillars of the University of Scranton

3.144 Lillian Thompson
Administrative Offices

Lillian Thompson's tale is woven into the fabric of the University of Scranton, a narrative as rich and intricate as the Ivy adorning the campus buildings. She hailed from a modest household in Scranton, her family rooted in the soil of Pennsylvania. Education had been her ladder out of the mines and into the university's administrative offices during the transformative era of the early 1970s.

As an administrative assistant, Lillian's days were structured by the rhythmic clacking of typewriter keys, the shuffling of paper, and the unending ringing of phones—a symphony of academia's daily grind. Her role was multifaceted, serving as the ligament connecting the various limbs of the university body. She scheduled, organized, and managed with a deft hand, ensuring the seamless operation of an institution in the throes of progress.

The work environment reflected the times—dynamic yet constrained by the era's technological limitations. The Catholic identity of the institution permeated the air, a silent guide in the ethos of service and community. Lillian's desk was a hub of activity, situated in the administrative heart where the secular and the sacred met.

Unsung Pillars of the University of Scranton

Challenges were as constant as the change of seasons. Budgets were tight, and the expectations were high. But Lillian's triumphs were etched in the small victories—the successful events, the crises averted, and the students who went on to shine. Her resourcefulness became a legend whispered in the corridors.

The relationships Lillian fostered were her most authentic legacy—ties of mutual respect with her colleagues, bonds of affection with the students, and a rapport of cautious admiration with the management. She was a fixture in the university's narrative, a comforting constant in an era of flux.

Lillian's reflections on her role were a tapestry of pride and reflective contemplation. She found fulfillment in the knowledge that her work was a cornerstone in the grand design of education. Intertwined with her vocational duties, her faith lent her a sense of purpose that transcended the mundane.

Like Ivy's soft but persistent growth, her impact was silent yet memorable. Her dedication was recognized in the subtle nods of appreciation, the quiet words of thanks, and the occasional commendations that found their way to her desk.

Within Scranton, Lillian's role symbolized the steady, unseen forces that drive a community forward. Her job, though behind the scenes, was a thread in the city's vibrant tapestry, connecting the university's Catholic mission to the secular needs of the town.

As the decades have passed, Lillian's memory lingers in the university archives, the stories passed down to new generations of staff, and the alum reminiscences. Her legacy is the enduring spirit of diligence and dedication that she imparted to the very ethos of the university.

Unsung Pillars of the University of Scranton

The historical context of the 1970s, with its societal upheavals and cultural shifts, was a backdrop to Lillian's tenure at the university. The Catholic institution stood as a beacon of stability and tradition amid the changing tides.

Reflecting on those years, one might ponder the stark contrasts with today's digital, fast-paced world. Yet, the essence of Lillian Thompson's story remains timeless—the human element in education, the unquantifiable impact of a job done with heart, and the enduring nature of a community's gratitude. Like the institution she served, her story is a testament to the lasting value of dedication and the human touch in shaping minds and nurturing spirits.

Unsung Pillars of the University of Scranton

3.145 Carmella Verdetto
Residence Halls

Carmella Verdetto might not have made the headlines, but within the walls of the University of Scranton, her presence was a constant in the ever-changing flux of academia. Hailing from a modest background, typical of the hardworking families in Scranton, Carmella's education may not have reached the heights of the scholars who roamed the same halls. Still, her wisdom was rooted in the reality of everyday life. Her journey to the university's residence halls was not through scholarly ambition but through the necessity of sustaining a livelihood.

As a domestic employee in the early 1970s, Carmella's role was integral yet often invisible. Her duties encompassed the upkeep of the living quarters, ensuring that the students' second homes were kept clean and welcoming. It was a routine of sweeping, mopping, dusting, and the occasional comforting word to a homesick student. Each day was a repetition of the previous one, but within that repetition lay a rhythm that brought order to student life.

The work environment was a dichotomy of the traditional and the academic avant-garde, shaped by the Catholic identity of the institution. This identity was an undercurrent in every aspect of university life, perhaps more so for the staff like Carmella, whose

Unsung Pillars of the University of Scranton

life was likely intertwined with the church, reflecting the standard cultural fabric of Scranton.

Working with limited technological resources and budget constraints, the job was physically demanding and often went unnoticed. Yet, Carmella's contributions resonated silently through the floors' polish and the laundered curtains' crispness. The triumphs were not in grand achievements but in the seamless invisibility of her work; when everything was in its place, students could pursue their studies without worry.

Her relationships with others at the university were likely as varied as the tasks she performed. Management might have recognized her diligence with a nod or a word of thanks, while co-workers shared the camaraderie of shared burdens and small victories. Students might have been oblivious to her toil or seen in her a maternal figure who cared for their living space as they navigated college life.

The personal reflections of someone like Carmella about her work would be complex. There might have been pride in her resilience and the independence her job afforded her, mingled with frustration at the lack of recognition. Yet, there might also have been a deep sense of satisfaction, knowing that her work, though behind the scenes, was the backbone of the institution's daily life.

Her efforts were likely felt more in their absence than in their presence. A clean room is seldom noted, but a dirty one is immediately apparent. Her appreciation came not in awards but in the smooth running of the halls she maintained.

Carmella's role in the community of Scranton was not just as an employee of the university but as a member of a predominantly

Unsung Pillars of the University of Scranton

Catholic society, where work reflected one's character and contribution to the community. Her position might have been modest, but it was respectable, embodying the era's ethos.

Carmella's legacy is one of continuity and care, a testament to the many who work silently to support grander missions. She is remembered in the polished surfaces, the orderly corridors, and the comforting consistency that nurtured thousands of students.

Set against the backdrop of the 1970s, with its societal upheavals and the shifting tides of education and religion, Carmella's story is a slice of the era's tapestry. Working in a Catholic institution then, she might have been part of a more homogeneous cultural landscape, quite different from today's diverse and technology-driven campuses.

Carmella's vignette reminds us that every cog in the wheel plays a part in the movement of the whole, and every story, no matter how seemingly small, contributes to the larger narrative of a place and time.

3.146 Joan Volinsky
PBX (Switchboard)

In the woven fabric of Scranton's history, Joan A. Volinsky is a thread of a steadfast hue. She hailed from the bustling streets of New York, carrying with her the resilient spirit of her Roman Catholic upbringing and the educational foundations laid in the local schools of her youth. In her heart was a melody of the family life she cherished, harmonizing with the hum of the telephone lines she would come to know well at the University of Scranton.

As a telephone switchboard operator in the early 1970s, Joan's role was pivotal yet often unseen. Her voice was the first greeting many heard, a gentle guide through the maze of academia. The cords she plugged in and the buttons she pressed connected thoughts, ambitions, and hearts across the campus. It was a dance of precision and patience, one she performed with grace amid the trill of rings and buzzes.

The Catholic identity of the University was not just a backdrop but a resonance with her faith, adding a layer of kinship to her daily tasks. The walls of the switchboard room, lined with the technology of the times, were a far cry from the digital ease of today, yet Joan navigated them with an expert touch.

Unsung Pillars of the University of Scranton

Challenges were many—technological hiccups, the occasional flood of urgent calls, and the unending need to be precise and quick. But Joan found satisfaction in the rhythm of her work, in the appreciation from management and the students whose lives ran smoother due to her diligence.

In the tapestry of the institution, Joan's threads crossed with many—colleagues who shared whispered laughs during brief moments of quiet, students who only knew her voice but felt the warmth it carried, and faculty who relied on her steady presence. There was a camaraderie in the shared mission, a sense of being part of something greater, a community striving toward enlightenment.

Joan's reflections on her work were as varied as the calls she fielded—pride in her efficiency, frustration at odd hours, and a profound sense of fulfillment. She was more than a switchboard operator; she was a caretaker of connections, a guardian of the gateway to knowledge.

Her impact was like ripples on a pond, outwardly invisible but vitally important. Recognition was not her pursuit; it was the silent knowledge that her role, though behind the scenes, was the linchpin of the University's daily pulse.

In Scranton, her work was a quiet testament to the role of support staff in an academic institution's life. The local community saw her as one of many who kept the heart of the city beating, a part of its Catholic core, and a member of its broader social fabric through her additional roles at the Lackawanna Medical Group and Rite Aid stores.

Unsung Pillars of the University of Scranton

Joan's legacy is one of unwavering reliability, a reminder of the human element in a world increasingly ruled by technology. She is remembered for her voice, her dedication, and the subtle yet significant part she played in the lives of those around her. Her story is a chapter in the University of Scranton's history, marked by the steady clicks of a switchboard now silent.

The 1970s were a time of change, social upheaval, and technological advancement. Joan's experiences were framed by this era's unique challenges and opportunities. Working in a Catholic institution then was to be immersed in a world where faith and education were deeply intertwined, a contrast to the more secular approach often seen today.

Joan A. Volinsky's narrative is a vignette of a bygone era, a personal account that, while singular, reflects the collective memory of a community and an institution navigating the currents of time. Her journey from the New York schools to the switchboard at the University of Scranton is a testament to the quiet yet crucial roles that shape our shared history.

Unsung Pillars of the University of Scranton

3.147 Peter Walsh
Saint Thomas Hall

In the heart of Scranton, in the shadow of the grand Saint Thomas Hall, a man of simple means but rich character worked tirelessly. Peter Walsh, a name not etched in stone but woven into the lives he touched, hailed from a family where grit was inherited, and education was a luxury they afforded through sacrifice.

Employed as a maintenance man, Peter's days were filled with the hum of fluorescent lights and the clank of wrenches against the stubborn pipes of the aging hall. His role was as much a guardian of the premises as it was a caretaker of student welfare. From sunrise to sundown, Peter toiled, ensuring that the heat ran through the old building's veins during biting winters and that each corner of the campus was a testament to order and care.

The University of Scranton, a Catholic institution, was not just an employer but a community Peter served with a silent reverence. The Catholic ethos was not just in the crucifixes on the walls but in the service of its staff. Peter's work, often unseen, was a quiet sermon of dedication.

The 1970s brought challenges: economic strains, social upheavals, and a technological metamorphosis. Yet, Peter's resolve was unyielding. His hands repaired what broke, and his presence was a constant in an era of change. The tools may have been rudimentary, but his craftsmanship was nothing short of skilled artistry.

Relationships were the actual currency for Peter. His exchanges with co-workers were peppered with banter, a shared joke here, a helping hand there. The management knew him by name, and the students knew him by the safety and comfort he provided. His satisfaction did not stem from accolades but from the nods of acknowledgment as students passed by, the warmth they felt in their rooms, a testament to his behind-the-scenes labor.

In Scranton, a town where every person's role was a thread in the community tapestry, Peter's job was modest but vital. The status was not in titles but in trust and dependability. He was as much a part of the city's heartbeat as the church bells that rang every hour.

His legacy? Not in monuments but in the reliability of the brick and mortar he maintained, in the seamless days on campus that spoke of his attention to detail. He was part of a narrative more significant than himself, a chapter in the university's storied history.

Reflecting on that era from today's vantage point, one sees a chasm in technology and social norms, yet the essence of dedication remains timeless. Peter's work in a Catholic institution of the early 1970s was a testament to a universal truth: that labor, offered in sincerity, transcends the bounds of time, and its echoes are felt long after the hands have stilled.

Unsung Pillars of the University of Scranton

3.148 Thomas Walsh
Estate

In the heart of Scranton, among the reverent halls of the University, toiled a man by the name of Thomas Walsh. His hands, rough and capable, spoke of the honest work of a maintenance man. It was in the early 1970s when Thomas found his calling amidst the ivy-covered buildings of the Jesuit Residence, affectionately known as 'the estate.'

Hailing from a lineage sturdy as the Pennsylvania coal mines, Thomas carried the humility of his family's working-class roots. Though not extensive, his education was rich in life's lessons, taught by the rhythm of seasons and the value of hard work. The University of Scranton, a beacon of Catholic values, became his employer, his charge, and, in many ways, his sanctuary.

As the sun crested the Pocono Mountains, Thomas's day would begin. His role, while frank in the title, was vast in responsibility. From the humming of boilers to the creaking of ancient pipes, he was tasked with ensuring the heartbeat of 'the estate' never faltered. His daily dance with wrenches and pliers was a silent testament to the institution's ceaseless pursuit of academic excellence.

The estate's venerable walls echoed with scholarly debate and Jesuit discourse, a place where faith met reason. In his silent way,

Unsung Pillars of the University of Scranton

Thomas contributed to this dialogue not through words but through the meticulous care he gave to every lightbulb that changed every polished floor.

The challenges were as constant as the chime of the campus clock tower. Budgets were tight, and the day's technology was as stubborn as the winter chill. Yet, Thomas navigated these trials with the ease of a seasoned mariner, his triumphs not in accolades but in the seamless continuity of campus life.

His rapport with others was built on nods and smiles, a shared joke with a professor, and a word of advice to a homesick student. The staff and students may not have known the depths of his thoughts, but they felt the warmth of his presence, a reassurance as constant as the northern star.

In moments of quiet reflection, perhaps Thomas found a sense of fulfillment. This Catholic institution, with its grand mission, was more than a workplace; it was a testament to a community's spirit, and he was its steadfast guardian.

Thomas did not seek recognition, but it came in the form of grateful nods, the relief of a warm classroom, and the joy of a well-lit study hall. His impact was as pervasive as the autumn leaves graced the campus grounds.

Thomas's legacy was not etched in stone but in the memories of those who walked the estate halls. His dedication was a silent, enduring thread in the University's rich tapestry.

The 1970s, a time of change and upheaval, perhaps seemed a world away within the sanctuary of the campus. Yet, people like Thomas Walsh grounded the University of Scranton in an unwavering reality in its commitment to service and community.

Unsung Pillars of the University of Scranton

And now, as we reflect, we see not just a maintenance man but a custodian of history, a man whose story is a reminder that every cog in the machine is vital. In the changing times, from then to now, the essence of such work remains the heart of an institution's success.

3.149 Isabelle Williams
Estate

Isabelle Williams' story is a mosaic of silent corridors and the murmurs of earnest conversations, a tapestry woven into the fabric of the University of Scranton's history. Born into Scranton's coal-dusted breath, she carried her town's resilience in her quiet demeanor. Her hands, though worn, were a testament to the diligence that was as much a part of her as her name.

Isabelle's journey to the Jesuit Residence, known as the estate, wasn't marked by fanfare but by necessity. The education she forwent in her youth became the lessons she learned amidst the hallowed halls, her knowledge shaped not from books but from the polished wood and stone she tended to daily. Her role, while uncelebrated in the annals of academia, was pivotal. As a domestic in the early 1970s, Isabelle's days were filled with the swish of a broom, the clink of china, and the silent swiping of dust from ancient bookshelves.

The estate itself was more than just a residence; it was a repository of spiritual pursuit, where the Catholic identity was as pervasive as the ivy that clung to its outer walls. For Isabelle, this identity was a double-edged sword that commanded respect and imposed silence. Intertwined with her labor, her faith was evident in the care she bestowed upon the priests' quarters, the

Unsung Pillars of the University of Scranton

reverence with which she handled the clerical vestments, and the quiet "God bless you" that followed the sneezes of theologians.

Challenges were manifold; the technological simplicity of the era meant everything was manual. The absence of modern conveniences was not a hindrance to Isabelle but a measure of her capability. She found triumph in the gleam of a well-waxed floor, the crispness of laundered linens, and the grateful nods of passing scholars.

The relationships she formed were the silent symphony of her workday. There was camaraderie in shared duties, a silent pact among those who toiled behind the scenes. Yet, appreciation was often a whisper, overshadowed by the louder accolades given to academic achievements. Management, ensconced in administrative duties, seldom saw the ligaments of the institution's daily life, where Isabelle and her colleagues were the unseen heartbeats.

In the eyes of the Scranton community, Isabelle's role was humble yet essential. Her position was not one of status but of service, a role that resonated with the town's working-class ethos. At church, her presence was another quiet affirmation of her dedication to her work and her community's spiritual foundation.

Isabelle's legacy is not etched in stone monuments but in the echoes of her influence that linger in the estate's timeworn rooms. Though not enshrined in plaques, her memory is preserved in the minds of those who knew the worth of her contributions and who felt the warmth of the residence she maintained so faithfully.

The 1970s were a backdrop to her narrative, a time of social upheaval and economic change. Yet, within the estate's walls,

Unsung Pillars of the University of Scranton

Isabelle's world was constant, buffered from the tumult outside. And while technology, social norms, and the role of religion in education have dramatically transformed, the essence of service that Isabelle's life epitomized remains a timeless thread in the university's ongoing story.

In a time when the role of religion in public life was more pronounced, working at a Catholic institution like the University of Scranton was to live within a confluence of faith and labor, a blend that Isabelle navigated with grace. Her reflections were to be voiced, perhaps speaking to a simpler time when the lines between duty, belief, and community were indelibly drawn yet harmoniously intertwined.

Unsung Pillars of the University of Scranton

3.150 Louise Wilson
Graduate Office

In the brisk air of Scranton, among the rustle of papers and the steady click of typewriter keys, Louise M. Wilson found her stage. Born into the warmth of a close-knit family, her journey led her to the heart of the University of Scranton's Graduate Office in the early '70s. As a secretary, Louise became the unseen hand guiding the administrative pulse of academia. Her days were spent scheduling, typing dissertations in triplicate, and serving as the nexus between students and faculty in a bustling educational world.

The University, a Catholic institution, stood as a testament to tradition and the pursuit of knowledge. In this place, Louise's work ethic shone like the stained glass of Christ the King church, where she found solace and community. The faith-based ethos of the University permeated the walls, offering both solace and a framework for the morality infused within her daily tasks.

Challenges were as frequent as they were varied—from the now-archaic mimeograph machines to the constant pressure of deadlines and the ever-present need to stretch the meager office budget. Yet, Louise navigated these with a grace that belied the difficulties, her successes often unsung but no less vital.

Unsung Pillars of the University of Scranton

Her rapport with others was built on respect and a shared purpose. Whether it was the camaraderie with fellow staff, the appreciative nods from management, or the grateful smiles from students, Louise's role was a thread in the University's tapestry, her subtle and profound impact.

Louise's reflections on her work might have been a mosaic of pride and quiet satisfaction. In a time when women's roles were rapidly evolving, her position at the University was both a job and a statement—a testament to her dedication and an embodiment of the changing face of the workforce.

Her role might not have been headline-making in the community, but it was undoubtedly backbone-forming. Scranton knew her as one of many who kept the cogs of progress turning. At Christ the King's church and within the hallowed grounds of Cathedral Cemetery, where she rests, her legacy endures in the memories of those she touched.

The '70s framed her world—a time of shifting cultural tides and emerging technologies. Yet, within the halls of the University of Scranton, Louise's legacy is not bound by the era's constraints but rather by the timeless influence of her diligence and spirit.

Louise M. Wilson's story is one of quiet strength, a narrative woven into the broader history of a community and an era. It's a vignette of a life that ended too soon and left an indelible mark on the fabric of an institution and the hearts of those within it.

Unsung Pillars of the University of Scranton

3.151 Judy Wotanis
Cafeteria

In the bustling heart of Scranton, amongst the hum of the early '70s, worked Judy Wotanis, an emblem of diligence at the University of Scranton's cafeteria. A local through and through, Judy's roots were steeped in the coal-dusted pride of Pennsylvania, her family echoing the town's hardworking ethos.

While steeped in routine, her days were a whirl of activity - bread slicing, stirring hearty stews, and clanging pots and pans. She was a familiar face behind the steam and sizzle, serving up sustenance and smiles to a tide of students. Her role, though unheralded, was crucial: she fueled the minds that would one day lead.

The cafeteria, with its long tables and the echo of shared stories, was more than a feeding ground; it was a place where the pulse of the university kept time. The Catholic identity of the institution was not just in the crucifixes on the walls but in the shared values of service and community. Judy's work, in its essence, was a quiet testimony to these principles.

Challenges were part of the daily menu - the limited technology of the time meant everything had a personal touch, which, while charming, also demanded more. Budgets were tight, but Judy's ingenuity ensured no student left hungry. Her triumphs were in the small victories, the satisfied nods, and the empty plates returned.

Judy's rapport with her colleagues was built on the unspoken understanding of shared goals. Management knew her worth, fellow staff shared her toils, and often-homesick students found comfort in her maternal presence. She was part of the fabric of the place, woven into its history with threads of dedication.

Reflecting on her days, Judy's heart swelled with a complex brew of pride and yearning. There was pride in her role in nurturing generations, yet a yearning for what more could be done. The university was her mission field, her service a silent sermon.

Her impact was like the steady flame under a simmering pot - not always seen but deeply felt. Recognition was not her aim, but it was as warming as her homemade soup when it came. She was appreciated by the nods of professors, the students' gratitude, and her peers' respect.

Judy was a part of Scranton's community tapestry, her role at the university a single, significant thread in the city's broader social weave. In a time when the town's fortunes were as much a subject of prayer as effort, she represented the steadiness of the Catholic spirit in everyday life.

Today, Judy's legacy lives not in grand gestures but in the collective memory of those she served - a legacy of constancy and care. Her story is a chapter in the university's history, reflecting a time when the personal touch was the most advanced technology and community was the strongest currency.

The '70s were a time of change, yet within the hallowed halls of the University of Scranton, some things remained timeless - like the service of Judy Wotanis. Her experience at a Catholic institution was a testament to the enduring nature of faith and service, contrasting the swift currents of change in today's world. Judy's simple yet profound story mirrors an era where work was more than a job - it was a calling.

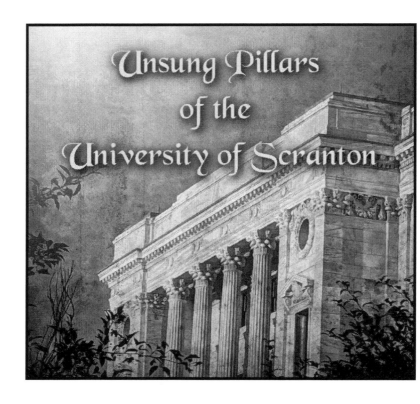

Chapter Four

Echoes of Excellence: The Lasting Legacy of Scranton's Stewards

Unsung Pillars of the University of Scranton

In the final chapter of our homage to the support and administrative staff of the University of Scranton in the early 1970s, we step into the corridors of history, where the echoes of past endeavors mingle with the whispers of progress. Here, amidst the timeless brick-and-mortar of an institution that has weathered the flux of decades, we find an enduring spirit—a commitment to excellence that was both the hallmark and the foundation laid by those who served in 1972.

As we leaf through the pages of this book, filled with 151 biographical vignettes, we are reminded that each person was a thread in the vibrant tapestry of the university's culture. Their individual stories, rich with dedication, weave a collective narrative of resilience and unwavering service. Each shaped the university's destiny, from the unseen custodian who polished the floors to a reflective sheen to the administrative assistant whose fingertips danced with proficiency across typewriter keys.

The early 1970s were a time of profound change and challenge. The world was transitioning with cultural revolutions, political upheavals, and the relentless march of technological innovation. Yet, within the embrace of the University of Scranton, the support staff remained a steady force. Their contribution transcended the mere performance of duties; they were the quiet custodians of tradition, the unsung heroes fostering an environment where academic pursuits could thrive.

Today, as we traverse the same halls they once did, we sense their legacy in the meticulous records that chart the university's growth, the meticulously maintained grounds that have hosted generations of scholars, and the smoothly run systems that are the lifeblood of an academic institution. Their legacy is not etched in stone but in the living ethos of the university—an ethos that champions the pursuit of excellence.

Unsung Pillars of the University of Scranton

It is a legacy that teaches us that the accurate measure of our work is not in the noise it makes but in the silence of efficiency and the satisfaction of well-done tasks. It tells us that while times may change, the essence of commitment remains immutable, a guiding star for those who follow.

As we close this book, let us not see it as an end but as a beacon. For as long as there is a commitment to excellence in the work products of their descendants, the spirit of the support and administrative staff of 1972 continues to live. They set the path for the future, not by grand gestures but by their daily dedication to the university they served.

Let us honor them in words and by emulating their dedication to excellence. Every spreadsheet that is meticulously analyzed, every event that is seamlessly executed, and every student whose life is quietly improved by the smooth functioning of this great institution, their legacy lives on.

We stand on the shoulders of these giants, not colossal in their renown but monumental in their contribution to the fabric of the University of Scranton. As we move forward, let us carry their torch high, passing on the flame of commitment to excellence to the next generation just as they have passed it on to us.

In the end, the true testament to their impact is not just in the visible achievements of the university but in the unseen excellence that underpins every aspect of its life. Their work was often behind the scenes, but their influence is front and center in the university's reputation as a bastion of educational excellence.

The legacy of the support and administrative staff of 1972 is a silent yet potent force—a dedication to quality, a commitment to service, and a passion for the greater good that continues to guide the University of Scranton. As we honor their past, we also lay the groundwork for a future that continues to be inspired by their ethos of excellence.

And so, we thank the support and administrative staff of yesteryears. Your work has been the wind beneath the wings of this institution. May we, who benefit from your legacy, continue to fly ever higher, buoyed by the same spirit of excellence you embodied.